IMPRESS
FAITH
ON YOUR KIDS

Mark Holmen

randall house

14 Bush Rd I Nashville, TN 37217
randallhouse.com

© 2011 by Mark Holmen
Published by Randall House
114 Bush Road
Nashville, TN 37217

All Scripture quotations are taken from The HOLY BIBLE, NEW INTERNA-TIONAL VERSION®. NIV®. Copyright© 1973, 1978, 1984, 2010 by International Bible Society. Used by permission of Zondervan. All rights reserved.

Printed in the United States of America

13-ISBN 9780892656127

Acknowledgements

I would first like to acknowledge and give thanks to Jesus Christ, my personal Lord and Savior, for opening the door for me to write this book. Like the Apostle Paul I feel like I am "less than the least" when it comes to being qualified to write a parenting book yet I praise God for giving me a "repetition of the law" through Deuteronomy 6 and for inspiring me to share this message with others.

I also praise God for my wife, Maria of over 20 years and my wonderful daughter Malyn who both allow me to speak and write openly and honestly about our experiences as a D6 family. I love you both and thank you for your faithfulness to God and the Faith@Home message that He has given us to spread all over the world.

I would also like to give God thanks and praise for the people at Randall House who have made this book possible. What I appreciate the most about each of you is the fact that you are friends and true partners with me in the D6/Faith@Home movement that God is leading.

And finally, I would like to acknowledge my mom as well as the Ellison families; Ray and Sue, Mark and Erin as well as Matt and Kerry. Without your love, prayers, encouragement and support I couldn't be serving God's Faith@Home movement full time and writing books like this. Thank you.

Table of Contents

Introduction

Deuteronomy 6:7, as well as the entire chapter of Deuteronomy 6, is very personal to me because I am now devoting my life to teach, preach, write, and speak about it literally all over the world.

In the fall of 2009, I gave up my position as the senior pastor of a large church in southern California to become a full-time missionary to the Faith@Home movement. This movement is a movement led by God through the church to reestablish the home as the primary place where the Christian faith is lived, nurtured, and expressed. As a missionary to this movement, I have the opportunity to travel all over the world to speak to parents and church leaders about how to be more Faith@Home-focused individuals and churches. Throughout the past few years, it has been truly amazing to watch thousands of parents come forward to make commitments to be more Faith@Home-focused parents; and the message they are responding to is not *my* message . . . . it is the message of Deuteronomy 6.

Therefore, I feel it is important for me to express that I firmly believe the words I write or speak have little or no power or authority to change or impact anything in your life. Yet God's Word has the power to move mountains, which means that His words and instruction not only can impact your life, but also the lives of your children and grandchildren! If anything in this book impacts you or your family for the better, give God the credit because God alone deserves all the praise.

As the one that God has called to write this book, I am very excited to take you on a journey into a passage that has literally changed me as a man, husband, father, youth pastor, and senior pastor. My prayer is that God will use the words on these pages to speak His truth into your life in a way that only He can. All I ask is that you remain open to hearing what God has to say in the pages that follow.

I don't believe in coincidence, and yet, I am a firm believer in "Godincidence." Simply stated, I believe God has a plan and purpose and there is a reason this book has ended up in your hands at this time. I don't know where you are in your parenting journey. I don't know where you are in your spiritual journey either. You may have come from a Christian household that lived out Deuteronomy 6 in your home; but more likely you grew up in a home where there was little or no spiritual conversation or behavior at home. You may have a strong family that is functioning well right now or you may be struggling to simply survive. You may be a two-parent household, a single-parent household, a grandparent raising grandkids, or you may have just had your first child. You may be a strong, devoted, life-long Christian or you may simply be someone who doesn't know much about God at all but you're at least willing to see if He has something to offer you. At the end of the day it really doesn't matter where you are in your parenting or spiritual journey because it's a new day and God has given you this book to read now. Why? I don't know, but God does. So let's just take this journey together and see where it leads!

P.S.—Letters to . . .

As an author, you are instructed to have an audience in mind when writing a book. Recently, God put someone in my path who has truly impacted my life and given me "the person" to whom I will be writing.

My friend is a great guy in his early-to-mid thirties. He is married with two young children under the age of six. He has been a successful businessman, but with the recession has found himself, like many, having to downsize and diversify in order to maintain a sustainable income. Unfortunately, in the midst of these trying financial times, he has also found himself going through marital difficulties. The trauma in his marriage is excruciatingly painful for him; yet he has done an incredible job handling himself and his children through the process. My friend is clearly committed to his children, protecting and caring for them as his top priority. However, my friend is not a Christian, at least not yet. This does not mean that he doesn't know God or right from wrong. He does, and he readily admits he believes in a "higher power."

What I respect most about my friend is his ability to share his thoughts and feelings through lengthy e-mails or letters. While this is not a normal skill for most men, he clearly has a gift for communicating through these personal letters that clearly depict and convey the thoughts and feelings on his mind and heart.

As I prepared to write this book, my friend was obviously on my radar and heart. I believe it was a "Godincidence" that we would spend so much time together prior to my writing. I realized my friend may never read this book; so I decided to write him a letter when I concluded each chapter. Thus, these "Letters to . . . " have been added at the end of each chapter.

I recently read a book with my daughter entitled, *READY*, by my friend Tim Smith. The book is intended for dads who parent teenage daughters about to enter high school. At the end of each chapter, Tim shares a letter he wrote to his daughter as she was preparing for high school. When my daughter and I went through the book, we found ourselves appreciating the letters most. Of course that doesn't mean there wasn't good stuff in each chapter; there was. But we simply found the letters gave us something to think and talk about in a more personal way.

I'm hopeful you won't skip the chapters in this book and only read the letters because I believe there is good stuff for you in the chapters as well. But for some reason God put it on my heart to also include these letters. My prayer is that these "Letters to . . . " will help to convey the truth God is speaking to you in more personal way.

In Christ's Service,
Mark Holmen

Chapter 1

Good or Bad Pudding?

My dad always used the expression, "the proof is in the pudding," which I understood to mean that the results would speak for themselves. In other words, if the pudding tasted good, then the right ingredients were used and it was made correctly. If the pudding didn't taste good, then the ingredients were wrong or the preparation was off. Nonetheless, the starting point, and ending point for that matter, was the taste of the pudding.

The starting and ending point of this book is to impress a genuine, authentic, and lasting faith in God on the hearts of our children. During the past 15 years of ministry, I have been blessed with the opportunity to work with thousands of parents. I can say with complete conviction that I do not believe we have bad parents today. In fact, I believe just the opposite: today we have parents who are absolutely committed to doing whatever it takes to be the best parents they can be, seeking to establish a more stable household than the one they grew up in. Why is that the case? Because the majority of young adults who are becoming parents today grew up in broken or dysfunctional families with marginally committed parents. As a result, they have seen first-hand the pain this can cause a child. Thus, many young adults today are waiting longer to marry and have children because they don't want to make the same mistakes their parents made.

I repeatedly hear this from new parents: "I am not going to put my kids through what I had to go through. I am going to be a better mom/dad than my mom/dad."

And that's my starting point. You don't want to simply be a good or average parent, but I believe you want to be the very best parent possible. Jim Collins in his book *Good To Great* writes, "It is possible to turn good into great in the most unlikely of situations. Greatness, it turns out, is largely a matter of conscious choice."[1]

Dad, I believe you want to be more than just a good dad. I believe you want to be a great, solid, committed, and respected father who is there for your children. Mom, I believe you want to be more than an okay mom. I believe you want to be a great, strong, stable, and life-giving mother for your children.

But WHAT would qualify someone to declare, "I'm a great parent"?

I'm a Great Parent if . . .

Many parents today believe "great parenting" simply means spending more time with your kids—going to more ballgames, attending more school activities, and helping more with homework. Or parents think it means providing more things for them like a better place to live, better clothes to wear, or a better school to attend.

We hear the term *deadbeat parent* a lot used to describe someone who is disengaged from his/her kids and/or does not pay his/her alimony. I guess that means a non-deadbeat parent is someone who engages with their children in some way and makes sure they have provided for the needed resources for success. Is that all there is to it? Am I a great parent if I spend a few hours with my daughter each week, attend a few of her activities each month, and provide money for her to have some of the essential things she needs?

These things may make you a better parent, but I'm not sure they ultimately lead to being great parents.

I know many great parents, who were not able to spend a lot of time with their kids, nor were they able to provide a lot of material things for them, yet they were still great parents. If spending more time or money on our children doesn't determine what a great parent is, then what does?

For me, defining or determining if someone is a great parent or not is really easy because the "proof is in the pudding".

See, I am setting before you today a blessing and curse—the blessing if you obey the commands of the LORD your God that I am giving you today; the curse if you disobey the commands of the LORD your God and turn from the way that I command you today by following other gods (Deuteronomy 11:26-28).

This day I call the heavens and the earth as witnesses against you that I have set before you life and death, blessings and curses. Now choose life, so that you and your children may live and that you may love the LORD your God, listen to his voice, and hold fast to him (Deuteronomy 30:19-20).

> **A great parent is one who leads his/her children into life not death.**

For me, a great parent is one who leads his/her children into life not death. Is that plain and simple enough? I think all would agree that any parent who knowingly leads his/her children into death is not a great parent. But on the other end of the spectrum is the opportunity to lead our children into life—eternal life. I don't think any sound minded parent would knowingly lead their children to death yet many parents do not realize that they have another option. A far better option. We can actually lead our children to a pathway that leads through death to eternal life and I believe great parents are parents who lead their children to follow this pathway. And what is the pathway that leads through death to everlasting life?

*For God so loved the world that he gave his one and only Son, that whoever believes in him **shall not perish** but have eternal life. For God did not send his Son into the world to condemn the world, but to save the world through him* (John 3:16-17, emphasis added).

Do you realize that death does not have to be the end for you and your children? Isn't that comforting to know? The key words in John 3:16 are "whoever believes in Him shall not perish but have eternal life." We have a chance to live after death!

Believe me, as a parent myself, I know your greatest fear—death of a child. I have been there too many times. The phone rings in the middle of the night, and it's a distraught parent on the other end of the line: "Pastor Mark we need you to come over right away. We are living a nightmare. We just received word that our teenager was killed in a car accident. Please come over. We don't understand why. We need your help. We don't know what to do or where to turn."

I've lived this nightmare with parents who have lost infants to SIDS, children to cancer, teenagers to drunken drivers, and adult children to suicide. Yet the great news of the Gospel is that death does not have to be the end for anyone, including and most important, our children.

God did something about death. He defeated it!

I have come that they may have life, and have it to the full (John 10:10).

Since the children have flesh and blood, he [Jesus] *too shared in their humanity so that by his death he might break the power of him who holds the power of death—that is, the devil—and free those who all their lives were held in slavery by their fear of death* (Hebrews 2:14-15).

God isn't some big bad guy in the sky waiting to judge and shame you every time you do something wrong as a parent. God is in your corner. God wants you, your children, and grandchildren to live joy-filled, blessed, and pain- and suffering-free lives forever! That is why God sent His one and only Son to defeat death because God is a parent like you; and like any great parent, God doesn't want any of His children to perish! Therefore, what makes for a great parent? A great parent is anyone who leads his/her children to life, not death, through faith in Jesus Christ.

Choose Wisely

Now you must make a choice. Are you going to be a parent who leads your children to life or not?

> *Now fear the LORD and serve him with all faithfulness. Throw away the gods your ancestors worshiped beyond the Euphrates River and in Egypt, and serve the LORD. But if serving the LORD seems undesirable to you, then choose for yourselves this day whom you will serve, whether the gods your ancestors served beyond the Euphrates, or the gods of the Amorites, in whose land you are living. But as for me and my household, we will serve the LORD* (Joshua 24:14-15).

I love this passage because it makes the choice very clear. Am I going to be the type of parent that follows God and His ways in such a sold out fashion that my children are so impressed by it they too decide to follow Christ, which ultimately leads to us enjoying eternal life together? Or am I going to be the type of parent that leads my kids to follow other worldly gods, which may bring them temporary rewards but ultimately leads to their death? What type of parent are you going to be and whom are you going to influence your children to love and follow?

The way you parent is going to influence who your children are and what they become. Let me say that again just to make sure you don't miss it: The way you parent is going to influence who your children are and what they become.

The world is offering you options (gods) as to the way you should parent. Unfortunately, the worldly ways/gods are attached to worldly outcomes that do not lead to life after death. The worldly gods have not and cannot defeat death. Only Jesus Christ has done this. Therefore you have a choice: live and parent God's way, which will lead you and your chil-

> **The way you parent is going to influence who your children are and what they become.**

dren to eternal life together, or live and parent the world's way, which will lead to death and permanent separation.

Now What?

If you are like most parents, your problem is not the choice you need to make. I can hear you say, "Hey Mark, I'm not an idiot or some sort of person who wants to lead my kids to death. I want to lead them to life. But I don't know how to impress faith on the hearts of my children?" The answer is in God's Word:

> *I lift up my eyes to the mountains—where does my help come from? My help come from the LORD, the Maker of heaven and earth* (Psalm 121:1-2).

The world is full of people who would counsel you on parenting your children. But I'm not going to give you any advice or counsel from them or any other secular source because we have a better source–the Bible.

The Bible is God's living Word to you from the one and only God who created you and your children and the same eternal God who wants you and your children to live together with Him forever. Why do I remind you of this? So that you understand where God's advice/counsel is coming from. Unlike talk show gurus, God is not trying to sell you anything nor does He have an ulterior motive other than the fact the God doesn't want any of his children, including you and yours, to perish. God doesn't care about the ratings nor does he worry about getting his book on the *New York Times* best sellers list (but the Bible has been the #1 *New York Times* best seller for 20-plus years!) God, through His Word, is simply trying to lead you and your children to life. His wisdom, counsel, and advice is personal, practical, and challenging; yet, if followed, will lead you and your family where you need to go.

> *For I know the plans I have for you,"* declares the LORD, *"plans to prosper you and not to harm you, plans to give you hope and a future* (Jeremiah 29:11).

Isn't it nice to know in advance where we are going? Our destination is to be great parents who lead our children to follow God and His ways, which ultimately leads to eternal life. God has given us everything we need in and through His Word to enable us to do that.

Repetition of the Law

The word *deuteronomy* means "repetition of the law." In Deuteronomy, the prophet Moses continually repeated himself as he addressed the Israelite nation. The Israelites, as God's chosen people, had been delivered from captivity in Egypt through the miraculous work of the Lord when He parted the Red Sea. That act enabled them to cross on dry land before the Lord brought the waters down on Pharaoh's army, who were seeking to destroy the Israelites.

Unfortunately, the Israelites' joy is short lived as they now find themselves in the midst of a long, difficult journey to the promise land (due to their disobedience). During this long journey, we find the book of Deuteronomy, which is a series of Moses' speeches and acts where he repeats the wills and commands of God to this very stubborn, unsettled, and disobedient group of people.

While the Israelites heard many of these truths before it seemed they had forgotten and fallen away into a lifestyle of disobedience. That reality required Moses to repeat the commands of God to them to return them to a life of commitment and obedience.

Does that sound familiar? Do you seem to recognize the ways of God when you hear them, but realize that you have fallen away again? In many ways we may need a "repetition of the law" more today than ever before!

As I have had the opportunity to work with thousands of parents throughout the years, I believe the vast majority of them know God's ways and commands. Now they may not be able to recite the Ten Commandments, but they know

> **In many ways we may need a "repetition of the law" more today than ever before!**

that murder, using God's name in vain, committing adultery, and stealing are all wrong. They also know we should be a people committed to prayer, worship, and giving of our time, talent, and treasure to the Lord. The problem is: We parents just don't want to follow them because we are stubborn, unsettled, and disobedient.

I was recently talking with a friend who was wrestling with how he could become a more devoted follower of God. At one point he said, "I just wish God would clearly tell me what to do, and I would do it."

Friends, when it comes to hearing from God and knowing God's ways, there is good news. God reveals His will through His Word. God is telling us what to do through the truth of the Bible. The problem is we don't listen or follow what the Bible teaches.

Deuteronomy 6 is instruction from God on how to be wise parents. This chapter is one of the most recognized and recited passages of the Old Testament because it is part of the "Shema," which is considered to be one of the most important prayers in Judaism. It is traditional for Jews to say the Shema as their last words each day, and parents to teach and recite it with their children before they go to sleep at night. The Shema is so important that most Bible scholars say it was likely the first Scripture Jesus learned as a child. In fact, when Jesus was later asked what the most important commandment was, without hesitation He quoted part of the Shema.[2]

Therefore, as we go through Deuteronomy 6, you may not find new information, advice, or counsel. In fact, you will probably discover you already know or have heard most of it before, yet you simply needed to be reminded, or better stated, kicked back into gear.

If this is the case for you, please know you won't be the first nor will you be the last who needs a repetition of the law. I probably teach on Deuteronomy 6 more than 50 times a year, and I still find myself going through life following and then falling away . . . following . . . and falling away. I still need a "repetition of the law!" Thankfully, I serve a God of infinite chances who continues to be patient, faithful, and forgiving with me even in my times of unfaithfulness. And that same God has been faithfully waiting for you as well.

So there is our starting point. We all desire to be great parents. A great parent is defined as someone who leads his/her children to life not death through faith in Jesus Christ. Yet we recognize that we need help in knowing how to lead our children to life. Thankfully, God has provided, through Deuteronomy 6, a repetition of the law for how we to accomplish this so we can enjoy eternal life with our children and grandchildren forever. Therefore, a good parent is a D6 (Deuteronomy Six) parent who leads their children to life!

Small Group Discussion Questions

1. Finish the sentence: A great parent/mom/dad is someone who . . . .
2. How would you describe your parents growing up? What did they do well and not so well?
3. In what ways are you parenting in a similar or different fashion as your parents?
4. Who or what did your parents influence you to be and follow?
5. Who or what are you influencing your children to be and follow currently?
6. What do you think of the definition that a great parent is someone who leads his/her children to life not death?

Letter to . . .

Greetings my friend,

How's life treating you? Still hanging in there? I know these past few weeks have not been easy for you; yet I want you to know I feel you are handling yourself incredibly well considering all the things thrown your way lately that you had no control over. Most guys I know would have "blown it" in some way, but you have remained strong throughout this time. I just wanted you to know this is something I greatly respect in you.

I still marvel at the fact that less than a year ago we hardly knew each other and now we find ourselves as close friends going through a very difficult life situation together. Your friendship is something I really appreciate. I know it will continue to grow deeper in the years ahead, no matter which way things go, as long as you never beat me at golf! You do know that will never happen, right? I mean, seriously, I get to golf year round, and you only get to play a few months out of the year. I digress.

The reason I'm writing this letter, and the letters that will follow in the weeks ahead, is because I want to share some things with you that I'm not sure how else to present because of the distance between us. Ideally, I know we will one day have a conversation about this sitting by your campfire but for now this will have to do. So here goes.

Obviously, in addition to me being a great golfer (I just can't stop), you know that I'm a devoted Christian and that my faith and commitment to doing life God's way is central to who I am. Does this mean I'm perfect? Not even close as you can attest, but I would not be a true friend to you if I didn't share the following. I believe and know that you are a great guy who is also a great dad. You have a huge heart, and I know you want to be the very best dad you can be, especially in the midst of the trials you are facing. In the book I'm writing, I started by defining what I believe makes for a great parent. Obviously the world will say a great dad is someone who is there for his kids, listens to them, encourages them, and provides for them. I'm sure those are all well and good; but at the end of the day, I think we have a much greater purpose than that as dads.

As you know, everyone is going to die. I don't know about you, but I feel like death cheats everyone, even someone in their 90s because it sure seems like we were created for much more. I mean we have minds that can learn much more and a whole universe yet to explore; so why are we limited to just 80-90 years on earth? Well, the fact of the matter is, that we were created for more. We have a God who has given us a chance for more—a chance to live beyond death, a chance to explore the vastness of everything He created with our children and grandchildren in a place where there is no pain, suffering, or death. God does not want death to cheat us from having that, so God did something that only God can do—defeat death and create a pathway to eternal life. How did He do that? I want you to look at this one passage from the Bible, which is probably the most important thing you will ever read.

> *For God so loved the world* [which means you and your children] *that he gave his one and only Son, that whoever believes in him shall not perish but have eternal life. For God did not send his Son into the world to condemn the world, but to save the world through him* (John 3:16-17).

As you are probably aware, for Christians, Easter is a time when we celebrate the fact Jesus rose from the dead, which is a HUGE deal because that was God defeating death for all of us! Now, as a result of His resurrection, all we need to do is believe in Him and follow His ways so as to lead ourselves and our children and grandchildren into LIFE! Therefore, I define being a great dad as someone who leads his children to life not death. In other words, as I think of the type of dad I am to my daughter Malyn, am I going to be the type of parent that will lead her to follow God, which leads to her eternal LIFE, or will I be responsible for leading her not to follow God, which leads to DEATH?

I realize this is heavy and a lot to handle so let me close this first letter with the following thing for you to consider. You can be the nicest guy in the world, who is seen as a really cool dad in the eyes of your children, but how would you feel if you later found out that you were responsible for leading them to death when you could have led them to life? I KNOW YOU, and I know you would never knowingly lead your kids to death when you could have led them to life. That's why I couldn't keep this from you. What type of friend would I be if I kept this information from you? Therefore I'm simply inviting you to con-sider joining me on this journey of following Christ and leading our children to follow Him so that we may all enjoy eternal life together . . . and golf as much as we want in heaven together, which would give you time to get better and beat me! (Just had to get that one last golf shot in there.)

I love you like a brother. Thanks for letting me share this with you.

In Christ,

Mark

Chapter 2

Do This So That . . .

M y wife and I have moved 11 times in our 20 years of marriage. Let me tell you, moves are not easy. Most of our moves happened in our first 12 years of marriage, but our last move happened in the fall of 2002 when we moved from Minneapolis, Minnesota to Ventura, California. Of all our moves this one was, by far, the longest and hardest transition because it meant traveling more than 1,500 miles and leaving all of our friends and family in the Midwest to live in a city we had only visited twice.

The process of being called to the senior pastor position of Ventura Missionary Church was a very exciting time for us because God made it very clear this was where He wanted us to serve as a family. Yet after the decision was made and everyone was informed, we then entered a time of transition where we need to conclude our ministry at the church in Minneapolis and begin our move to Ventura.

I would like to say that during that time of transition we never doubted our decision, but that would not be accurate. On numerous occasions we found ourselves saying, "Are we sure this was the right decision?" We hardly knew anything about Ventura. Now we were going to live there and raise our daughter there? We didn't know anyone there. We didn't have a house, and the cost of housing was daunting. We often wondered if we should rethink this whole decision. Yet, in those times of doubt, God would always do something through a well-timed phone call, e-mail, or conversation with someone to reassure us that we were doing exactly what God wanted us to do.

For many parents the idea of becoming a D6 household is a move into "different." Maybe you're still not sure you want to make this move; or maybe you've made the decision, but now you're wondering if it was the correct decision. Maybe you jumped in too quick? Maybe you should reconsider?

God knows you feel this way so be reassured through Deuteronomy 6:3 "Hear, Israel [insert your name here to personalize this passage], and be careful to obey so that it may go well with you and that you may increase greatly in a land flowing with milk and honey, just as the LORD, the God of your ancestors, promised you."

Assurance #1: So That It May Go Well With You

If you are like most families, you have been searching for wellness as a family. When we hear the words, "so that it will go well with you" this captures our attention.

God wants things to go well for your family. Many parents possess a completely wrong impression of who God is—some big judge in the sky frowning upon or zapping them whenever they do something wrong. That's not our God. We have a God who loves us and has done everything in His power to show us the way we need to live so that life will go well for us. He wants us to obey so that life will go well for us. That doesn't mean life will be *easy*, but it can still be *well* even in the difficult times.

In the fall of 2002, my dad was diagnosed with a pulmonary fibrosis and pulmonary hypertension, which as a combination meant he would only have about two years to live. My dad was more than a father to me; he was also my mentor, friend, and only other male confidant in our family. My dad introduced me to golf, horseback riding, boating, cars, ministry, and most important, Jesus Christ. My dad was a camp director for more than 20 years who loved to give kids from the inner city of Chicago a chance to come to a week of camp. My dad also had a huge heart for mentally challenged adults, making it possible for them to attend camp as well. My dad was loved by the thousands of campers and hundreds of camp counselors he mentored. Many people remember him as "Uncle Arlie" the crazy Caucasian camp director who would drive his camp bus into Cabrini Green, one of the most dangerous projects in the inner city of Chicago, to pick up kids for camp.

I had just begun my transition to California when we received the news about my dad's condition. Of course, this was very difficult for me. I didn't want my dad to die in two years. I didn't want to see him suffer. I wanted him around for me as I began my new adventure as a senior pastor. Yet there was nothing that could be done, and the disease progressed.

During his final few months, we had a last boat ride together in my boat. When I offered, dad took the wheel, as he always did, and drove from lake to lake standing at the wheel as I sat in the back seat and held back tears. The ride was incredible, and none of us could believe how well dad did. But when we got back to the dock, my dad collapsed into my arms out of fatigue as he got out of the boat. Life wasn't easy, but it was still well for us.

A few months later, I received a call from my mom saying they had taken my dad to the hospital in Minneapolis and it didn't look like he would have much more time. I was on a plane within hours. When I showed up in the hospital, there was my dad sitting in his hospital bed with his oxygen; yet, when he saw me through his mask he smiled and greeted me with a huge hug and kiss. A couple of nights later I volunteered to be the one who would stay with dad so my mom and sisters could get a good night's rest. During the evening, a college age gal came by to visit my dad. I didn't know her but my dad instantly recognized her as one of his former confirmation students from five years earlier. As they visited, she shared that she was now in college majoring in religion and that is was my dad who gave her the desire to go into the ministry. As she prepared to leave, she gave my dad a hug and tears flowed from her eyes because she knew this would be the last time she would see him this side of heaven. But my dad sat up in his bed, grabbed her by the hand, and as he looked her directly in the eyes with a huge smile on his face he said, "Don't grieve for me. Life is good because God is good." Losing my dad was one of the hardest and most painful things I have ever faced in life, but it was still "well."

Life is going to happen to all of us. But if we continue to "obey" God, He promises it WILL go well with us. I have seen life happen to hundreds of families in all sorts of devastating ways, and yet the families who have made it through were families who continued to obey.

Assurance #2: And That You May Increase Greatly

A second assurance that God gives is that God also wants you and your family to increase greatly. In other words, God doesn't want things just to go average for you as a family. He wants things to get better for you. God wants to move you from good to great as a family! There are specific things that God wants to increase in the life of your family. They are what the Bible calls the "fruit of the Spirit" which are love, joy, peace, patience, kindness, goodness, faithfulness, gentleness, and self-control (Galatians 5:22). Could you use a little more of these attributes in your family?

Take a moment to assess which fruit you currently have in your life and/or family and which fruits you would like to see "increase" in the future? (Put an X next to those you have, and circle those that you would like to see appear or grow more heartily in the future.)

_____ Love   _____Joy   _____ Peace

_____ Patience   _____ Kindness   _____ Goodness

_____ Faithfulness   _____ Gentleness   _____ Self-Control

The good news is that God promises that D6 families will "increase" greatly! Those are two really good reasons why we should "be careful to obey" God's ways as D6 families: "So that it may go well with you" and that you may "increase greatly."

A Transition Process

As is the case with any move, it takes awhile not only for the move itself, but also to become comfortable in your new environment. In the same way, becoming a D6 family is a process—it takes time.

No matter where you are in the transition process, I simply want to say: Hang in there because being a D6 parent and family will be worth it! If you are "careful to obey," it will "go well with you" and you will "increase" in love, joy, peace, patience, kindness, goodness, faithfulness, and self-control; and you will inherit eternal life! Be assured, in deciding to be a D6 family, you have made the right decision that's more than worth it!

Transition #1: A Move

When we announced to our families about our move from Minneapolis to Ventura, California, let's just say the reviews were mixed. Don't get me wrong, everyone was excited for us, but we were, at the time, taking the only grandchild with us. This made things more difficult for everyone.

In the months leading up to our move, we received all sorts of advice from people. I'll never forget my father-in-law's parting words: "You guys be careful, you hear me. It's a different kind of crazy out there."

While I'm not so sure Ventura, California is crazier than anywhere else, we do need to realize we all live in a crazy world filled with all sorts of things that can hurt or divide us as a family. The move to be a D6 parent may seem like a big move for you that some of your friends and family may question but God wants you to be completely assured that you have made the no doubt about it right decision.

Transition #2: A Journey

The second reason God wants us to "be careful to obey" is that life as a D6 parent is not an instantaneous fix but an ongoing journey. I'm a Star Trek fan, and I have always wanted a transporter so I could be beamed instantly from one location to another. Unfortunately, there is no such thing as a transporter, meaning I still need to drive or fly to my destinations. As you know, traveling takes time.

When I drove from Minneapolis to our new home in Ventura, California, there were times I wondered if I would ever get there. Thankfully, my map showed me that I was getting closer each hour. That knowledge made it easier for me to endure the trip.

When it comes to becoming a D6 family, we need to realize this too will take time. It's a journey that has a lot of opportunities for us to make wrong turns which is why we need to "be careful to obey" so that we don't wander around aimlessly or end up lost.

Transition #3: A Plan

So as D6 parents we need to start by being careful to obey the ways of God. The question becomes how do we do this? When I headed for California I didn't just start driving west without any plan for how I was going to get there. We have plans for all sorts of things: savings, retirement, maps or GPS, and even a grocery list. However, when it comes to planning how we are going to "be careful to obey," we have no written plan for that. How do you know you are "obeying" God as a family, if you haven't identified commandments and truths to follow?

To help with that, I would like to show you how to put together a written plan as a family so you can begin your journey towards becoming a D6 household. For my family it's what we call our family mission statement: (I'm not sure if the term *mission statement* best describes what we came up with because for us it is more of a target we are shooting for as a family). Here is our family's mission statement.

The Holmen family is a Christian family who:

Unconditionally loves, supports, nurtures and forgives each other.
Demonstrates fiscal responsibility, including giving of our time, talents, and treasure to the Lord.
Models faith and Christ-like living through what we think, say, and do.

Let me be clear before you think more highly of us than you should. Is this mission statement who we are on a moment-by-moment, day-by-day basis? I wish! Yet this is our mission and what we are seeking to be as a family. Through this mission statement, we can check on a regular basis to see if we are getting there.

For example, usually around the New Year holiday, we sit down as a family to read through our mission statement again. During that meeting, we spend time reflecting over the past year to see how we did. We identify ways we got better, but more importantly, we identify areas where we need to improve. Next we put together a simple strategy for how we will work on those issues.

This year we identified that we needed to improve our service to Christ through family service. Our weekly effort was an idea that came from our missions pastor: the trash-can-make-a-difference project. We placed a garbage can in our kitchen that has the trash-can-make-a-difference bumper sticker on it, and each week we fill it with items for a different mission or service organization. One week we are gathering food items for a local food pantry; and the next week it's diapers for our local pregnancy crisis center. When the trashcan is full, we as a family deliver the goods to the mission or service agency. On a monthly basis, we work at one of our area homeless shelters where we serve food, distribute clothing, or just help out with odd jobs. Finally, for our yearly project, we decided to go on a family mission trip to an orphanage in Mexico.

Your Family Mission Statement

In many ways, your family mission statement is your family's building plan. Whenever you build a house you need to put the plans together first and the plans need to be approved by someone before you can start building. Imagine trying to build a house without any building plans? No plans for the plumbing, electrical, foundation, or structural aspects of the home. How do you think the house will turn out? I feel a lot of families are struggling today because they are trying to build their family without a plan. A target, a goal to focus on can help. Here's how families can put together a mission statement:

Step 1: Individually list your non-negotiables.

On a sheet of paper, in individual bullet form using as few words as possible for each item, answer the following questions. Again, be sure to do this individually and include your children if they are at least five or six years of age.

- What do God-following families do?
- What do they not do?
- For me, we are a godly family when we . . .

Step 2: Make a master list.

- Share your lists with one another.
- Move the items that you all agree are important to a separate sheet of paper. This will become your master list.

Step 3: Put it into sentence form.

- Take the items from your master list and put them into a sentence structure using multiple identified items in each sentence.
- If you can't get it all to work/fit, then walk away from it and come back to it again in a day or so. This process may take a few days to accomplish.

Step 4: Evaluate it.

You know you have a good family mission statement if it:
- Will stand the test of time and won't need changing.
- Will hold you accountable.
- Will be something Jesus would approve of.

Step 5: Engrave it.

- Get your family mission statement engraved on a plaque to place in a prominent area in your home.
- As you hang your family mission statement in your home, take a moment to pray over it as a family asking for God's help to "increase" you in the areas you have identified on your family mission statement.

Step 6: Annually revisit it.

- Identify an annual time that you will sit down as a family and review your family mission statement.
- Recognize the ways you have grown and fulfilled your family mission statement over the past year.
- Mutually determine one or two areas where you would like to "increase" as a family in the next year.

    1. Identify something you will do once a week to increase in that area.
    2. Identify something you will do once a month to increase in that area.
    3. Identify something you will do once a year to increase in that area.

So there you have it! Now you have a customized plan that you are moving toward as a D6 family. If you have ever built a house you know the mixed feelings you have when you submit the final building plans. On one hand you are excited because you have carefully designed the home, yet right alongside those feelings of excitement are feelings of uncertainty. Are we really going to like the colors we picked? Should the bedrooms have been bigger? In the same way, we can have feelings of excitement and uncertainty about our new family mission statement. God is fully aware of our fears and uncertainties. Please know that no two families are the same. Don't compare or critique your family mission statement against others. Simply follow and obey the unique plan God has given you so life may "go well" and you may "increase greatly" just as the Lord has promised.

Small Group Discussion Questions

1. How many moves have you made as a family?
2. How big of a move will it be for your family to become a D6 family?
3. What scares/worries you about this move?
4. What excites you about this move?
5. How "careful" are you at obeying the ways of God? What helps and prevents you from being careful?
6. When you look at the "fruit" that will be produced, which ones do you need the most?
7. This week, work on your family mission statements. Bring them to next week's gathering and share them with one another.

See a Family Mission Statement template provided by the author on page 95.

Letter to . . .

So what's up, my friend? How is life treating you and your family? I have some questions for you to ponder. Have you ever wondered where you are going as a family? In other words, what is your plan or target as a family? What are you trying to achieve with your kids? If you think about it, we have retirement plans, savings goals, and business plans, yet when it comes to what we want to achieve as a family or with our kids, we have no plan for that. How crazy is that?

Did you ever wonder about God's plan for you and your family? Essentially God's plan, if you follow it, is to increase love, joy, peace, patience, kindness, goodness, faithfulness, gentleness, and self-control in your family, AND to lead you to enjoy long life, which includes life after death. You may be wondering why I am so convicted to follow God, and also, be so pushy on you as well; that's okay, I can take it. It's simply because I want both of our families to grow in love, joy, peace, patience, kindness, goodness, faithfulness, gentleness, and self-control and live forever in heaven.

So that being said, I have a homework assignment for you this week. (When was the last time you did homework?) I want to help you write a family building plan that can guide you to become the family that achieves the things listed above.

Step 1: Individually, you and your wife, list on separate sheets of paper without input from each other (which will be hard for you!) your non-negotiables. I would suggest you consider completing the following sentences by listing simple one or two bullet items for each. Feel free to include your kids in the process as well if you think they are old enough to answer these questions. You may be surprised by their answers!

- What is absolutely important to me is that we are a family who . . .
- A godly family to me is a family who . . .
- A godly family to me is a family who does not . . .

Step 2: When you are finished, which may take a couple of days, come together and share your lists with each other. As you do, take the items that you agree on and put them on a new, master list.

Step 3: Now put this list into sentence form, which again may take a few days. For example, here is our family building plan. Before you look at it, you need to know that you can't steal our plan! Just like each house has a unique plan, each family needs a plan that uniquely fits it.

The Holmen family is a Christian family who:

Unconditionally loves, supports, nurtures, and forgives each other.

Demonstrates fiscal responsibility, including giving of our time, talents, and treasure to the Lord.

Models faith and Christ-like living through what we think, say, and do.

Step 4: Before locking in your family building plan, ask yourself three questions: Will this plan be good over the long haul? Will it hold us accountable as a family? Would God approve of it? If the answer to all three questions is "yes," then you have a good family building plan.

Step 5: Get this plan engraved on a plaque or some sort of wall hanging and then display it in a place of prominence in your home. Don't be a cheapskate on this; do it well because this is the plan that will help you enjoy long life as a family.

Step 6: Finally, on a yearly basis, sit down as a family and read through your family building plan and identify:

- Where you have done well over the past year.
- Where you need to improve in the next year.
- And specific things you can do to get better in the next week, month, and year in your identified area of weakness.

I can't wait to see what you come up with. I will give you a week to get this done. Just kidding. Take your time and enjoy this next step in your journey to becoming a great family.

In Christ,

Mark

Chapter 3
Don't Do This

Looking Back . . . (Repetition of the Law)

- You want to be a good parent. A good parent is someone who leads his/her children to life not death.
- Deuteronomy 6 provides a roadmap for how to be a parent who leads your children to life, which is why we want to be D6 parents.
- D6 parents are "careful to obey" the ways of God so that "it may go well" and so that we may "increase" as a family.
- How do we do this?

An ineffective approach to D6 parenting is what I call a drop-off—letting the professionals do it, an outsourcing approach to parenting and impressing faith on your children. This parent takes the kids to church or Christian school and expects others to expose them to godly living and thinking.

I believe you are the parent and no one can replace you or be more effective than you. When it comes to a life versus death issue, I wouldn't think you would want anyone else doing that anyway, right? Yet, unfortunately, many parents today have abdicated the faith formation responsibility to the church or a Christian school by enrolling their children in church programs in the hope that these things will lead them to be Christians. That approach, as you will see from the data to follow, has proven to be, at best, minimally effective at impressing a lasting faith on our children. Do you want to be a minimally effective parent?

What I'm Not Saying

Before I go any further, let me make sure you understand what I'm *not* saying. I am not saying that enrolling your children in church programs, a Christian school, or sending them to Bible camp is a bad thing. I'm not saying you are a bad parent if you do these things, nor am I saying that these things can't lead your children to faith in Christ. These are good things that can lead your children to faith in Christ. I grew up at a Bible camp so I fully understand and have experienced firsthand the impact a week of Bible camp can have on the faith life of a child/teenager; so I would never say that a church program, Christian school, or Bible camp cannot lead your children to follow Christ. Yet, as you will see in the information and data that follows, this "drop off/outsourcing approach," where you expect church programs to be the PRIMARY influence that will lead your kids to a lifelong faith, is only minimally effective. Essentially, this approach will, in all likelihood, lead your children to enjoy Christianity for a period of time but not necessarily for the long haul. In other words, while your kids will participate and enjoy these church programs, and even come to have faith in Christ through these programs, the statistics and data that follows will show that, unfortunately, this approach does not seem to have a lasting impact that leads to a faith that stays with them as they mature into adulthood. In fact, the majority of children enrolled and participating in church programs today are going to disengage from their faith as young adults.

> The majority of children enrolled and participating in church programs today are going to disengage from their faith as young adults.

The Allens

I'll never forget the Allens. George was a leader in our church who served in many areas of the church, including on the governing board. His daughter Lisa was an active teenager who was involved in youth program. The Allens would be what I consider a very strong Christian family.

One afternoon I received a phone call from George asking if I could get together with him to discuss some issues he was having with Lisa. George said, "Pastor Mark, I simply don't know what to do. Lisa isn't listening. All she does is get mad at me, and she seems to be continually pushing the boundaries as far as she can go and then some. What should I do?"

What happened next was an exchange I'll never forget. I simply said, "George, it sounds like things are not good between you and Lisa. I can tell it's tearing you up because she is your precious little girl who's growing up. Have you prayed with her about this?"

By the look in his eyes you would have thought I just spoke a foreign language. "Lisa and I have never prayed together" George replied. "Do you actually think that may help?"

I was thinking to myself, "Are you kidding me? George has never prayed with his daughter? They are one of our most active families in the church? How can this be possible?"

To complete the story, when Lisa came home after practice, George took her out for dinner and later that night they prayed together for the first time. Their relationship was instantaneously restored and continued to be strong to this day!

Unfortunately, what I experienced with George and Lisa has proven to be normative in most Christian households.

- A study conducted in 1980 called *Young Adolescents and Their Parents* involved a national random sample of 8,000 adolescents whose parents were members of congregations in 11 different Protestant and Catholic denominations. The study showed that "God, the Bible, or religious things" are seldom discussed in church homes. **Only 10 percent of church families discussed its faith with any degree of regularity; in 43 percent of the homes in these denominations, faith is never discussed**.[3]

- A similar study conducted in 1986 involved 7,551 students from 196 randomly selected Catholic schools. When asked how often their family talks about religious things, **only 17 percent of the student claimed to discuss such topics at least once a week.**[4]
- In 1990, a national sample of youth and adults from six major Protestant denominations was asked the same question. Their response was no better: **35 percent of the youth, ages 16 to 18, said they rarely, if ever, talked about faith or God with their mother, and 56 percent reported not ever having such discussions with their father**. When asked how often they have devotions or worship as a family, 64 percent reported that their family rarely or never did so. **Only 9 percent reported holding family devotions with any degree of regularity.**[5]
- In a typical week, **fewer than 10 percent of parents who regularly attend church with their kids read the Bible together, pray together (other than at meal times), or participate in an act of service as a family unit**.[6]
- In a Search Institute study of more than 11,000 participants from 561 congregations across six different denominations the following results were revealed:
  - **Only 12 percent of youth have a regular dialog with their mother on faith and/or life issues.**
  - **Only 5 percent of youth have a regular dialog with their father on faith and/or life issues.**
  - **Only 9 percent of youth have experienced regular reading of the Bible and devotions in the home.**
  - **Only 12 percent of youth have experienced a servanthood event with a parent as an action of faith.**[7]

My friend and mentor, Dr. Dick Hardel summarized these finding by stating, "As is obvious from these percentages, faith sharing is not happening today in most families of the church. It seems as though parents do not recognize their role in the faith growth of their children.[8]

Let me reiterate, I do not believe we have bad parents today. I don't think you want to be a bad parent. Yet when it comes to doing what we need to do to lead our kids to life, through faith in Christ, I don't think parents have any idea how important their actions and behaviors at home are. Actually, I believe most parents who want their kids to know and follow God actually believe the best way to do this is to find a great church with great programs. Many parents make sacrifices to get their children to church programs; and they even change churches if they don't believe the church they attend is offering enough for their kids. Unfortunately, while the intentions are good, the approach is simply not the best because a church-focused, outsourcing approach to faith formation does not produce the desired outcome we are looking for in the majority of cases.

What's the Big Deal?

What difference does it really make that we don't pray, read the Bible, or engage in any form of faith talk in our home?

The big deal is this: By not engaging in faithful living at home with your children, you are actually giving the wrong impression of Christianity that will, in all likelihood, lead your children to become indifferent about, at best, if not altogether disengaged from, the Christian faith as they grow older. As hard as it is to see, please look at the following statistics that confirm this to be true.

- The National Study of Youth and Religion, which included in-depth interviews with at least 3,300 American teenagers between ages 13 and 17, found that **most American teens who called themselves Christian were indifferent and inarticulate about their faith.** The study included Christians of all stripes—from Catholics to Protestants of both conservative and liberal denominations. **Though three out of four American teenagers claim to be Christian, fewer than half practice their faith, only half**

deem it important, and most can't talk coherently about their beliefs, the study found.[9]

- "It's clear that despite our best efforts—all our training, commitment, resources, and creativity—today's teenagers are just not getting who Jesus really is, or they're not getting enough of who he really is, or they're getting, literally, a fake Jesus. As a result, few of them are living passionately with Christ in their everyday life . . . . **Maybe 85 percent of youth-group teenagers aren't getting to know Jesus intimately at church."**[10]

- **Sixty-one percent of today's young adults, who had been churched at one point during their teen years, are now spiritually disengaged.**[11]

- The Southern Baptist Convention reports **they are currently losing 70-88 percent of the young people after their freshman year in college** . . . and may never come back.[12]

- In one study, **90 percent of youth active in high school church programs drop out of church by their second year of college.**[13]

- If current trends in the belief systems and practices of the younger generation continue**, in 10 years, church attendance will be half the size it is today.**[14]

When author David Kinnaman studied what 18-29 year-olds thought of Christianity for his book *UnChristian,* one of the things he discovered was that the majority of them felt Christianity was hypocritical. Eighty-five percent of young people who are not Christians had sufficient exposure to Christians and churches to conclude that present-day Christianity is hypocritical. This negative perception has been similarly expressed by young churchgoers: Almost half agreed that Christianity is hypocritical (47 percent).[15] I believe the reason why many 18-29 year-olds believe Christianity is hypocritical is because the version of Christianity they experienced growing up was something that was "done" only at church and not at home. I refer to it as a different version of a drug problem. On Sunday mornings, many of these 18-29 year-olds were "drug" to church where they were put into church programs, but when they went home, there was no faith talk, prayer, Bible reading, or any other form of Christian living. So for them, Christianity was just something where you act, dress, and behave one way at church and then go home and act, dress, and behave completely different. Whether we like it or not, in most young people's experience, the term "hypocritical" has become fused with Christianity. As a result, many of these young adults are walking away from Christianity, looking for "real" spirituality. The statistics show the increasing number of parents—mothers and fathers alike—who renounce their responsibility to be spiritual leaders in the home. This lack of responsibility comes at a high cost not only to children being neglected, but also to society as a whole.[16]

Let's Get Personal

Now do you understand why the drop off, one-hour-at-church-only "Christianity" does not lead our children to have a true faith impressed on their hearts for life? Do you see how failure to live out your faith at home can actually lead your children to later abandon their Christian faith, saying it is hypocritical? And if you will let me be personal for a minute—maybe for you that is the reason why you have struggled with the church and/or Christianity because you experienced this hypocritical living in your household growing up.

As I have stated before, I do not believe we have bad parents today; yet when it comes to knowing how to be D6 parents who authentically live out their faith at home, we simply don't know how to do this because the majority of parents never experienced this in their home growing up.

Nonetheless, our walk with God was never, as you will see in the next chapters, something that was intended to be "at church" focused. The good news is that parents and churches all over the world are now beginning to understand this. Thankfully, we have a chance to get back to doing it right and start a whole new trajectory for our children and grandchildren. As Jim Burns, author of *Confident Parent-*

ing writes, you can choose either to recover from your family's past or repeat it.[17]

One of the most difficult things for me personally as a former youth and family pastor is to look back and see how many of the teenagers that were in my youth program that have now walked away from Christianity. Believe me, it wasn't due to lack of effort on my part in making sure the programs they participated in were inspirational and convicting. Unfortunately, the few hours I had with them at church or in our programs simply could not compete with the hours of time they had living in non D6 environments at home. Essentially, when they were done with the youth group they were done with following God and God's ways.

Small Group Discussion Questions

1. What impact did church programs have for you and your faith?

2. How did attending church help or hurt your faith?

3. How did the statistics impact you? What surprised you?

4. What is your reaction to the statement by Dr. Dick Hardel: "As is obvious from these percentages, faith sharing is not happening today in most families of the church. It seems as though parents do not recognize their role in the faith growth of their children"?

5. Have you experienced Christian hypocrisy? How has it impacted you?

Letter to . . .

Greetings my friend,

How is this week treating you? Just want you to know that I appreciate the way you are maintaining a strong, positive, and steady attitude for your kids. They need that from you right now. You are doing a great job, which I know is not easy for you.

So are you ready for another letter? Have you had a chance to put together a family mission statement yet? If not, you still have time because this week I want share with you what I have found to be the wrong approach when it comes to leading your children to life through faith in Jesus Christ.

As a former youth and family pastor, I unfortunately experienced a lot of "fake" or hypocritical Christian parents. They acted and dressed the part on Sunday morning, but when it came to "being" a Christian the rest of the week with their kids . . . it wasn't happening. One of the most alarming statistics I have encountered is that less than 10 percent of parents who regularly attend church with their kids read the Bible together, pray together (other than at mealtimes), or participate in an act of service as a family unit. Every time I read that statistic I want to scream, ARE YOU KIDDING ME? That means that for the majority of church going people today Christianity is something you do at church and not at home or anytime else during the week. And the result of this hypocritical lifestyle is that many children enrolled in church programs today wind up walking away from their Christian faith later in life. To be perfectly honest, I almost can't blame them. It's almost no wonder when, for them, Christianity was something you pretended to be on Sunday mornings but never lived out at home the rest of the time. I'm sorry but that's NOT what it means to be a Christian!

A Christian Parent Is Not:

- Someone who puts his kids in a church or Christian school but never goes themselves.
- Someone who expects the church to teach his/her kids the faith.
- Someone who only acts/behaves like Christian at church and then lives completely different the rest of the week.
- Someone who never prays with his kids, reads the Bible with them, or engages in any form of Christian service with them.

I don't know what your experience has been, nor do I know how your parents raised you when it comes to church or Christianity, but that really doesn't matter at this point because this is about us. Now is our time to be in the parent seat. Whether our parents did it right or not, we can. That's what I intend to do to the best of my ability. I don't want to be a hypocrite in my daughter's eyes, nor do I want to be responsible for leading her to walk away from God. I don't think you want to be a hypocritical dad who leads your kids away from God either; so that's why I'm inviting you to join me in being the type of dad who lives your faith 24 hours a day, seven days a week and not just on Sunday mornings. Next week we'll start exploring what that looks like. Love ya, bro. Hope the golf game is good. Hit 'em long and straight!

In Christ,

Mark

Chapter 4
True Love

Looking Back . . . (Repetition of the Law)

- A good parent is someone who leads his/her children to life not death.
- Deuteronomy 6 provides a roadmap for how to be a parent who leads his/her children to life, which is why we want to be D6 parents.
- D6 parents are "careful to obey" the ways of God so that "it may go well," and that we may "increase" as a family.
- D6 parents recognize they cannot outsource or abdicate the responsibility of spiritual formation of their children to the church.

I'll never forget when I was asked to co-lead a workshop for parents of teenagers with Dr. David Anderson. The workshop was entitled, "How to Pass On the Faith to Your Teenagers." At that point in my life, I was a fairly new youth and family pastor and my daughter was only two-years-old. I didn't feel very qualified to be leading the workshop, so I simply began with some opening remarks and then handed it over to Dr. Anderson. He began by asking the following question: How many of you wish your teenager had a stronger faith? Every hand in the room went up.

Next he said, "Realize that what you are seeing in your teenager's faith, is in all likelihood, a mirror image of your faith." At that point,

I was looking for the exit hoping no one would hit me with a tomato! But then I looked at the crowd of people, and instead of being angry, they were nodding in agreement.

Are You In Love?

In our next portion of Deuteronomy 6, we discover what faith in God is all about: *Hear, O Israel* [Lisa, Mike, Suzanne, Victor]: *The LORD our God, the LORD is one. Love the LORD your God with all your heart and with all your soul and with all your strength. These commandments that I give you today are to be on your hearts* (Deuteronomy 6:4-6).

A D6 parent, first and foremost, recognizes there is only one, true God—Father-Son-Holy Spirit. This is a non-negotiable for a D6 parent. D6 parents don't fall for lies about other gods or ways you can get to heaven other than through faith in Jesus Christ because there is no other way; *Jesus is THE way, THE truth, and THE life* (John 14:6)!

Second, being a D6 parent is about living in a loving relationship with God. It's not about "doing" church or being involved in organized religion. A D6 parent is someone who is in love with God.

The question to answer is: Are you in love with God? If you want to get more personal, I would ask: Are you living in such a way that those who know you best would say you are in love with God? And if you want a true litmus test, ask your children to identify whom you are in love with and see if God makes the list.

> **Are you living in such a way that those who know you best would say you are in love with God?**

When my daughter was 13, I asked her that question. On our way home from school, I simply said: "Hey Malyn, I have a question for you today?"

"Ok, what's that dad?" she responded.

"I was just wondering whom you think I'm in love with?"

"Huh?" she replied, caught by surprise.

"This isn't a trick question, I was just wondering if you could tell me whom you think I'm in love with?" At this point I began to wonder if this was really a good idea because I have a very honest 13-year-old daughter. But in what became a defining moment for me, my daughter responded: "Well that's pretty easy, Dad. You're in love with God, mommy, and me."

As a parent who is trying to lead your children to know, love, and follow Christ, it comes down to do you know, love and follow Christ? That's why the most important commandment is for us to live in a loving relationship with God. Your relationship with God will be what influences them the most.

Consider this:

- No one has more potential than mom and dad to shape the spiritual life of a teenager.
- Scripture makes the point from cover to cover. A stack of research taller than a day-camp cooler supports the same conclusion.[18]
- Most children and teenagers reared by Christ-adoring parents become Christ-adoring young adults. Most children and teenagers reared by parents without Christ become young adults without Christ. Many children and teenagers reared in spiritually shallow homes become spiritually shallow young adults. Parents *will* lead children spiritually, one direction or another. The faith of the children almost always will mirror that of parents. Parents must decide if that is good news or bad news for their families.[19]
- In *Soul Searching*, Christian Smith summarizes, "Most teenagers and their parents may not realize it, but a lot of research in the sociology of religion suggests that the most important social influence in shaping young people's religious lives is the religious life modeled and taught to them by their parents."[20]
- Because this is uncomfortable territory for many of us, we tend to hope the church does the job. The church is there to help, but the primary focus is on parents taking the leadership.[21]

- The evidence clearly shows that the single most important social influence on the religious and spiritual lives of adolescents is their parents. Grandparents and other relatives, mentors, and youth workers can be very influential as well. But normally parents are most important in forming their children's religious and spiritual lives.[22]

- "For all their specialized training, church professionals realize that if a child is not receiving basic Christian nurture in the home, even the best teachers and curriculum will have minimal impact. Once-a-week exposure simply cannot compete with daily experience where personal formation is concerned."[23]

As you can see from these quotes, the influence of mom and dad in how they live in a loving relationship with God is the most important aspect in the spiritual growth of a child. To impress faith on our children God says it starts with YOU loving the Lord your God with all YOUR heart and YOUR soul and YOUR strength. As Delores Curran wrote more than 30 years ago: "We need to gather together the impressive data showing that the parent is the primary determinant of a person's faith, and present it over and over in every way possible until we convince parents of its validity. Until we do so, parents will continue to visualize themselves as adjuncts to the faith process. Adjuncts do not necessarily become responsible."[24]

Now What?

This now sets up an obvious question: How do I come to love God personally? Thankfully, Deuteronomy 6 provides the answer to this question. True love requires your heart, soul, and strength.

Your Heart

Loving God with your heart means that you have an emotional attachment or yearning for God. Are you drawn or connected to God emotionally?

I'll never forget when I saw the emotional love my wife has for our daughter. This happened when we were getting ready to put her on an airplane without us for the first time. We arrived at the airport two hours before the plane was taking off, sending our daughter to spend time with her grandparents. My wife, trying avoid getting emotional, found a way to talk about anything and everything under the sun. She kept herself constantly on the move never sitting down next to Malyn and myself. Finally the announcement was made for boarding to begin, and the stewardess came to escort our 13-year-old daughter to her seat. I gave my daughter a big hug and kiss and prayed with her, but in doing this, I stayed strong and positive with her so that she would not get overly emotional. This was difficult for me because I'm normally the compassionate and emotional one in the family, but I held it together nicely. Yet when it was my wife's turn, she did something none of us will ever forget. She lowered herself so that her face was directly in my daughter's face; and then she put both of her hands on either side of Malyn's head. As she began squeezing her hands together she stared intently into Malyn's eyes and as tears rolled down her cheeks she said, "Malyn, you need to know that I will always love you! Okay? I will always love you!" Poor Malyn had no chance or choice but to break down into tears.

True love is an emotional matter of the heart. Therefore loving God with your heart involves loving him emotionally as:

- Your *Father*—The love a parent has for his/her child is a heartfelt love like none other, as is the love a child has for his/her parents. Regardless if you have a loving relationship with your parents or not, you need to understand that you have a heavenly Father who created you, who knows you by name, who knows every detail about you, and who deeply loves you—no matter what! This truth should tug at your heart.
- Your *Savior*—God is more than your Father, He is also your Savior. What is a savior? A savior is simply someone who saves you from something. What is God saving you from? Death. Without God we have absolutely no way to defeat sin's curse of death. Yet God did something about it whereby he sent

His one and only Son, Jesus Christ to defeat death for us: *For God so loved the world* [which includes you and your children] *that he gave his one and only Son, that whoever believes in him shall not perish but have eternal life* (John 3:16). Through Christ's death and resurrection a way has been paved for all of us, who simply believe in Him, to live beyond death. That makes me love God! Anyone who would give His life to save my life, or more important, my daughter's life, has more than earned my heartfelt love.

Your Soul

While a heartfelt love is an emotional love, a soulful love is a life of love. In other words, it is a love that gives you life.

Many of us have heard the term *soul mate*, which I define as someone who completes you. In other words, you seem to connect and intertwine in such a way that you can't imagine doing life a part from one another. In fact you recognize that life without the other would leave you feeling vulnerable, weak, and incomplete.

When you love God with all of you soul, it's when you recognize God as your soul mate. It's more than emotional feelings; it is now a relationship that gives you life. Other relationships can come and go, but your relationship with God is what matters most to you because without it, you would feel vulnerable, weak, and incomplete.

As a pastor, I have been with people who have lost their spouse of more than 50 years to cancer, best friend to suicide, and five month old child to SIDS. Yet in all these situations, they stayed committed to their relationship with God. How was that possible? It's because they had more than a fleeting emotional connection with God. Their love for God was at the very core of who they were. It wasn't going away no matter what worldly catastrophe hit.

If you are like many people, you would like to have that type of soul mate relationship with God, but feel you are not "there" yet. As is the case with all relationships, the soul connection will require a little more time than the heart connection. When my wife and I first started dating our hearts were drawn together, but we weren't soul mates yet. After 20-plus years of marriage, I can definitely tell you that we have a deeper soul connection now than when we were dating.

Your Strength

To love God with your strength means your love for Him will persevere through good times and bad. Let me be clear, there will be times when loving God will not be easy.

Any married couple will tell you that falling in love was easy but staying in love required time, attention, and fortitude, if not outright stubbornness!

One of the best things our kids can see is the way we work on our marriage and our relationship with God. My daughter has watched my wife and I battle through all sorts of difficulties in our marriage, and there were many occasion when it wasn't pretty. Am I proud of that? No, and yet I am glad our daughter has seen the strength of perseverance in marriage.

True love is something you are willing to fight for and that takes strength I have had the opportunity to counsel many couples following a time of infidelity. Nothing is more difficult than when one spouse cheats on the other because it leaves the other one in a scary position—do you stay or do you divorce? When meeting with the spouse who has been victimized by the infidelity, I start with these questions: Do you still love your husband/wife? In other words, do you still feel an emotional connection to him/her (heart)? Do you still feel like he/she is your soul mate and the one who completes you (soul)? If the answer to these questions is yes, I then ask one final question: Do you feel you have the strength to fight for this marriage?

When you love someone with your heart and soul, it is only natural that you would also love that person with your strength and/or effort. We can't expect this love to grow or sustain without effort. God is continually putting forth effort to stay connected with us. Are we putting forth effort to grow deeper in our love for Him? How is God doing His part?

- God is always reaching out to us through His Living Word, otherwise known as the Bible. Are we reading it on a frequent or casual basis?
- God is always reaching out to us through His still, small voice, otherwise known as the Holy Spirit. Are we taking time to speak and listen to God through daily, or even more frequent, times of prayer?
- God is always reaching out to us through His creation, are we slowing down and even disengaging from the fast-paced world so as to connect to Him through the wonder of His creation?
- God is always reaching out to us through His bride, otherwise known as the Church. Are we spending time connecting to Him through worship and service to her?

Do these things require effort? Yes, but they will draw you closer to God. A true love for God is a love that is willing to do whatever it takes to stay in love with God.

Small Group Discussion Questions

Remember your children will love who you love. If you want them to love God, the best thing you can do as a parent is to love God with your heart, soul, and strength.

1. If you were to ask your children whom you loved, do you think God would make the list?

2. What is the most difficult aspect of living in a loving relationship with God for you? What is the easiest aspect?

3. How is your "heart" love for God? Do you feel emotionally connected to God?

4. How is your "soul" love for God? Do you feel that God is your soul mate?

5. How is your "strength" love for God? How strong is your love? What are you doing to make it stronger?

Letter to . . .

Hey, my friend!

How's life been for you? Probably better than me. Guess what I'm dealing with? My daughter is going to her very first homecoming dance! While she can't date until she is 16, she is still going to the dance with a "friend" along with about 21 other freshman. This whole high school scene has forced me to realize that my daughter is growing up, ARGHH! As I now look at every new relationship she has with more critical eyes, wondering if this person is good for her or not, and as she gets older, the more I am forced to realize that I'm not in charge of the relationships she will choose to have. So that only makes what we are talking about even more important.

What is your ultimate goal with your children? My ultimate goal with my daughter has been to raise her to love and follow Christ so that He will help her make wise decisions here on earth and so that she will one day enjoy eternal life. That's it for me. Does this mean I don't care about anything else? Not at all, I still have other hopes and dreams for her like making the Olympics in track (okay, maybe I'm setting the bar a little too high here, but that's what I'm supposed to do as a dad, right?); getting married to a Christian man (even though I'm contemplating raising the dating age to 30!); and one day having great kids of her own that we can spoil, who only live within a few hours of us.

But do you see the difference? Those are my hopes and dreams, but my goal is the ultimate outcome. I'm okay if Malyn doesn't make the Olympics, but I will not be settled or satisfied that I have done my job as a parent if I have not achieved my goal of leading Malyn to love and follow Christ so that we will enjoy eternal life together.

Now the question becomes: How am I going to achieve my goal? Thankfully, it's not as difficult as it may seem because it primarily comes down to one thing—our children will love who we love. I think this analogy will help me make my point.

One of your many flaws, my dear friend, is that you love the Minnesota Vikings (Da Bears!). It is unfortunately very clear to see your children already, at this very young, impressionable age, love the Minnesota Vikings. How did you do that? You simply loved the Vikings; and as a result, they love the Vikings. Where am I going with this?

There is something I now need to say to you as a friend that I hope and pray you will understand is coming from a place of love for you and your kids. Right now, I don't think your kids would say you love Jesus. As a result, they may never come to love Jesus either because of you. I don't think you want to be the reason they never know, love, or follow God to eternal life so that's why I'm being this direct with you. I think you want to be a good dad who leads your kids to life; therefore, I'm encouraging you to give a personal relationship with God a chance.

I realize that this may sound like an impossible bridge for you to cross, but I have a personal, loving relationship with God. If I can do it, anyone can! I also think you will find it much easier than you think. How do you get to know and love God personally?

- Get to know Him through reading His Living Word, the Bible. I would encourage you to read the Gospel of John as your starting point.

- Get to know Him by spending time with others who know Him well, which you will find at church. When you go, in addition to attending a Sunday morning worship service, please seek out places where you can get to know Jesus better. It may require that you attend a retreat or get into a Bible study or small group. Believe me, opportunities will present themselves and when they do . . . DO IT!

- Get to know Him better by turning to Him through prayer. Simply talk to God whenever you feel like it. Ask God questions, share your concerns with Him, and when something doesn't make sense, ask Him to give you wisdom and understanding.

- Get to know God by listening to His still, small voice when it speaks to you. Remember, whenever you have a chance to act there are usually two voices speaking, one that is telling you the right thing to do and one tempting you to do the wrong thing. Spend more time seeking, listening to and obeying the still small voice of God.

- And finally, please do all these things with your wife and kids! Don't leave them out; include them because they will help you see and know God in ways you wouldn't without them.

So that's our next step. If we want to be good parents who lead our children to life through faith in Jesus Christ, the best thing we can do is to love Jesus personally so that our children will love Him as well. This is a big step that will take time because building loving relationships can't be rushed. Take the suggestions I listed above one baby step at a time, and in due time, you will come to love Jesus with all of your heart, soul, and strength. I'm sure of that because I know Jesus, and I know you—you're a perfect pair! Thanks again for letting me share these things with you in such a direct manner. Feel free to call me if you have any questions.

Love ya, man.

Mark

Chapter 5
Impress Them

Looking Back . . . (Repetition of the Law)

- A good parent is someone who leads his/her children to life not death.
- Deuteronomy 6 provides a roadmap for how to be a parent who leads his/her children to life, which is why we want to be D6 parents.
- D6 parents are "careful to obey" the ways of God so that "it may go well" and so that we may "increase" as a family.
- D6 parents recognize they cannot outsource or abdicate the responsibility of spiritual formation of their children to the church.
- D6 parents know and believe there is only one, true God—Father-Son-Holy Spirit—and they live in a loving relationship with God.

When flying in an airplane, I prefer a window seat because I like to see things at this height. I also love when the airplane descends because the closer you get to the ground the more detail you can see.

As we continue to take our journey deeper into Deuteronomy 6, we are descending into the details of how to impress a lasting faith in our children.

We must keep in mind, as we lead our children to know, love, and follow God, that everything we do must come from a foundation of authentic love for God. The reason I emphasize this is because I have seen many families jump into performing a bunch of Christian rituals, as if that would be the key to changing their family. Yet, if we don't know why we are doing these rituals, then they simply become things to add to our "to do" list. For example, I have seen parents become more "spiritual" as a family by praying at every meal. Usually their prayer is a ritualistic prayer that they say the same way before every meal. Of course, I'm not against prayer before mealtime, yet if you don't know and love the God you are praying to, then these are simply words you are saying. They really don't have any meaning.

> **Our ritual is driven out of our relationship with God.**

Let me be clear: I am not against ritual. We ritually bless and pray with our daughter every evening. But our ritual is driven out of our relationship with God. We pray to God and seek God's blessing every night because we love talking to God and we want God's blessing. It is our relationship with God that drives us to do the things we need to do to be D6 parents.

Impress Them

Deuteronomy 6:7 says, "Impress them on your children."

The word *impress* in the original Hebrew literally means to establish, fix, or permanently brand like when a farmer brands his cattle. The brand is there for life.

In the context of Deuteronomy, God tells parents to "impress" the Ten Commandments upon their children—not literally branding them, but branding those truths in their heart and minds. Unfortunately, when most think of the Ten Commandments, they think of a list of rules or laws to follow or memorize and not a way of life to live joyfully and naturally.

Friends, the Ten Commandments and ways of God are not something we have to do, they are something we get to do. In Deuteronomy 6, God is not instructing us to memorize His commands or see them as something we have to do. To "impress them" on our children means they are to become an engrained part of who we/they are.

To help us do that let me show you how I personalized the Ten Commandments for my 15-year-old daughter:

Malyn, here are 10 things I pray will be so deeply engrained in you that you will always know and follow them without even having to think otherwise.

1. That you would know there is only one, true God: Father, Son, and Holy Spirit. "There is no God but one" (1 Corinthians 8:4).

Malyn, my hope and prayer for you is that you will always know there is only one, true God: Father, Son, and Holy Spirit and that you will spend your life getting to know Him better and following Him. No matter how unpopular it may seem or whatever pressure you may receive to consider other gods, I pray you will always stick with the one true God who loves you and has given His life for you.

2. That you would never disrespect God. "Do not swear falsely by my name and so profane the name of your God. I am the LORD" (Leviticus 19:12).

Hey kiddo, don't ever disrespect God or anyone else. I realize other people around you will swear, using God's name in vain, but I'm simply asking you to always be respectful towards God because God loves you and has given you life. He is worthy of your love, respect, and praise.

3. That you would always love to pray, worship, and read the Bible. "They devoted themselves to the apostles' teaching and to the fellowship, to the breaking of bread and to prayer" (Acts 2:42).

I pray that worship, prayer, and Bible reading will be something you will always naturally do and that you won't do these things out of obligation. I love to watch you worship, pray, and read the Bible because it shows that you are truly in love with God.

4. That you would always love and respect us as your parents, even when we fail you. "Children, obey your parents in everything, for this pleases the Lord" (Colossians 3:20).

I realize this may come across as self-serving, but I simply pray that we will always be close as a family. God put us together as a family for a reason. I truly thank God for you and mommy. May we always be a family that loves and respects one another. I pray that will be the same for you when you have children.

5. That you would not take revenge on those who hurt you. "'In your anger do not sin': Do not let the sun go down while you are still angry" (Ephesians 4:26).

I have always interpreted the "do not murder" commandment not only to mean the physical act of murder, but also to include not doing murderous things to others. Obviously, there are a lot of ways you could hurt someone. When we are hurt or angry, we are tempted to do hurtful things to others. Malyn, I truly wish I could keep people from doing hurtful things to you, but I can't. My prayer is that you will always choose the higher ground; that you will not return anger for anger; and that you will let God fight your battles. When people hurt you, give it to God and don't participate in some of the sinful things that Satan is tempting you to do.

6. That you would stay committed to being sexually pure. "Flee from sexual immorality" (1 Corinthians 6:18).

The world will constantly tell you it's okay to have sex with others before marriage and even to engage in affairs while being married, but as you know, that is not the truth. It's not okay; those behaviors lead to all sorts of problems and difficulties. The decision you have made to do it God's way will not be easy for you, but I'm here to say, stick with it! You're a great young woman who deserves a great man who will honor you and the decision you have made. If he doesn't want to honor you by waiting, then he isn't the right one for you. Flee from sexual immorality and temptation and you will be blessed.

7. That you would be honest and trustworthy. "Do not use dishonest standards when measuring length, weight or quantity" (Leviticus 19:35).

When the Bible says do not steal, I think it means not to always speak the truth and not take advantage of situations. Malyn, you will always be presented with opportunities to take shortcuts, cheat, or achieve results in a dishonest manner. Others around you will take advantage of those opportunities. I'm simply here to say don't do it and don't be afraid to call me or anyone else out for doing it either. Let's live our lives in a manner where we are above reproach, meaning we never have to worry if we might get caught for doing something wrong or dishonest.

8. That you would not lie or gossip. "A gossip betrays a confidence, but a trustworthy person keeps a secret" (Proverbs 11:13).

Essentially, this comes down to one thing—don't lie. Don't ever lie. Lies just get you into trouble. As a teenager, you are surrounded by liars. People will say lies about you, and you will constantly be tempted to lie. Let's be people who tell the truth in all situations.

9. That you would be content with what you have and who you are. "Godliness with contentment is great gain" (1 Timothy 6:6).

We live in a world that is always telling us we need to have more, become more, or achieve more. My prayer is that you will always be content with who you are, as you are! Obviously, I always want you to work hard as if working for the Lord, but please, do not let the pressure to have more take away your contentment. Be driven to do your best for God in what God has called you to do, but don't worry about what others have.

10. That you would continually avoid the temptations that come your way and that you would help others remain and not stray. "Put to death, therefore, whatever belongs to your earthly nature: sexual immorality, impurity, lust, evil desires and greed, which is idolatry" (Colossians 3:5).

Malyn, as you continue to grow and mature, there will be ongoing temptations you must put to death. It's something we all face in life. And as you go through life, you will encounter people who will be "tempters" and others who will be "remainers." Tempters will try to lead you to want and do things you shouldn't do, while "remainers" will try to keep you focused on being thankful for what you have and who you are in Christ. Let's make a pack to be "remainers" who encourage and strengthen one another and those around us. I will be your "remainer" and help you put to death your temptations, if you will be my "remainer" and help me put to death mine.

Of all the things I could impress upon my daughter is there really anything more important or valuable than these things? If our children have these 10 principles impressed on their hearts, imagine how those truths will impact who they are and the life decisions they will make! When these things are engrained in our children, they will lead our children to make wise, good, and godly decisions naturally. Unfortunately, when these things aren't engrained in our children, then it opens the door for them to engage in harmful or hurtful behaviors.

To help you become a D6 parent who impresses the Ten Commandments upon your children, let's take a moment to look at ourselves in the mirror to see how we are doing as parents and as a family. Remember, our children will know and love what we know and love. Use the following chart to identify how "impressed" these things are on you and your children.

Impress Them

On a scale of 1-5 indicate how strong each of these commands are impressed upon you and your children, with 1 being not impressed and 5 being strongly impressed.

Mom	Dad	Is This Impressed?	Child 1	Child 2	Child 3
___	___	You believe there is one, true God	___	___	___
___	___	You don't disrespect God	___	___	___
___	___	You pray, worship, & read the Bible	___	___	___
___	___	You love and respect your parents	___	___	___
___	___	You don't take revenge on those who hurt you	___	___	___

Mom	Dad	Is This Impressed?	Child 1	Child 2	Child 3
____	____	You are committed to staying sexually pure	____	____	____
____	____	You are honest and trustworthy	____	____	____
____	____	You do not lie or gossip	____	____	____
____	____	You are content with what you have and who you are	____	____	____
____	____	You flee from temptation & seek to be a "remainer"	____	____	____

Did you notice anything as you completed this? Are their similarities or parallels between the things impressed upon your hearts and what is coming out in your children? If you're like most families, you have some that are strongly impressed and others that may need work. That's okay. Remember, there is no perfect family; we all have work to do!

Small Group Discussion Questions

1. What were some principles and actions your parents impressed upon you?

2. What do you want to impress upon your children?

3. What has your past experience with the Ten Commandments been? What comes to mind when you hear the words Ten Commandments?

4. How did Mark Holmen's personalization of the Ten Commandments impact you?

5. Discuss what you discovered when you completed the Ten Commandment assessments.

Letter to . . .

Greetings, my friend,

How is fall treating you? Have you started getting out your Christmas decorations yet? I must admit one of the best parts of living in California is that I can decorate my entire house and yard without having to worry about how cold or snowy it is. And since I'm a complete nut for Christmas decorating, my work has greatly expanded now that I don't have cold conditions holding me back.

One of my favorite things about decorating for Christmas is seeing the way Malyn loves it as well. Each year, Thanksgiving weekend is our time to spend a good two days decorating the entire house, inside and out, for Christmas. We go crazy each year coming up with new ideas and ways we can decorate the house.

As parents we impress many things upon our children like the way Malyn has come to love Christmas decorating as much as me. When you think of all the things we can impress upon our children have you ever wondered what we should be impressing upon them? I mean, we can also impress the wrong things on our kids too. But what are the things we want to impress upon them? Here is a list of things I want to impress upon Malyn:

1. That she knows and believes that there is only one, true God—Father-Son-Holy Spirit.

2. That she doesn't disrespect God in the way she talks or lives her life for Him.

3. That she will pray, worship, and read the Bible on her own.

4. That she will always love and respect us as her parents.

5. That she will not take revenge on those who will hurt her.

6. That she will stay committed to being sexually pure.

7. That she will be honest and trustworthy in her dealings with others.

8. That she will not lie or gossip.

9. That she will be content with what she has and who she is.

10. That she will flee from temptation and seek to help others do the same.

Now where did I come up with these principles? These are the Ten Commandments that God wants us to impress upon our children. Unfortunately, we tend to think of the Ten Commandments as something we memorize or a list of rules we must follow instead of attitudes or behaviors we want to be engrained in our children.

Look at that list again and ask yourself: How do you think your kids would turn out, and how would life be for them if they lived according to these 10 principles? How would life be for us if we did a better job living according to these 10 guidelines?

While I'm glad Malyn has the same love for Christmas decorating as I have, at the end of the day, I would rather she have these 10 truths engrained in her because if/when they are, it will lead her to a better life not only now, but also forevermore! So how do we impress these Ten Commandments upon our children? By loving and living those ourselves. So let me get personal, do you:

1. Know and believe that there is only one, true God—Father-Son-Holy Spirit?

2. Not disrespect God in the way you talk or live your life for Him?

3. Pray, worship, and read the Bible on your own?

4. Love and respect your parents?

5. Not take revenge on those who hurt you?

6. Stay committed to being sexually pure?

7. Be honest and trustworthy in your dealings with others?

8. Not lie or gossip?

9. Be content with what you have and who you are?

10. Flee from temptation and seek to help others do the same?

Just so you know, I'm a work in progress in these areas, and yet, I'm glad I have these 10 principles to check myself against because I know the more I follow them the better my life will be. If you want, I would be glad to discuss the areas I'm working on if you want to do the same with me. Maybe we can both help one another in the areas where we are weak.

God bless you, my friend.

In Christ,

Mark

Chapter 6
Talk the Talk

Looking Back . . . (Repetition of the Law)

- A good parent is someone who leads his/her children to life not death.
- Deuteronomy 6 provides a roadmap for how to be a parent who leads his/her children to life, which is why we want to be D6 parents.
- D6 parents are "careful to obey" the ways of God so that "it may go well" and so that we may "increase" as a family.
- D6 parents recognize they cannot outsource or abdicate the responsibility of spiritual formation of their children to the church.
- D6 parents know and believe there is only one, true God—Father-Son-Holy Spirit—and they live in a loving relationship with God.
- D6 parents personally impress the Ten Commandments of God upon their children.

Since my family directed a camp, we had a lot of campers coming out of the inner city of Chicago. I had a chance not only to learn how to play basketball from them, but I also learned to talk the game as well.

My best friend lived on the west side of Chicago, and on numerous occasions, I would spend the weekend at his home. We both loved playing basketball, and getting to play on some of the outdoor courts on the west side of Chicago was an incredible experience for me as I was playing with some incredibly talented players. But when we played basketball, Curtis felt nervous.

I remember on numerous occasions Curtis saying, "It's not your play that makes me nervous because you can play with the best of them, but it's your talk that makes me nervous because you can also trash talk with the best of them." I must admit, while I could walk the walk when it came to holding my own on the basketball court, I could also definitely talk the talk.

Did you ever notice that you tend to talk about the things you love? For example, I love my Chicago sports teams. During baseball season, I talk about the Cubs; during basketball season, I talk about the Bulls; and when it's football season, it's all about "Da Bears" in my household.

Talk About It

Deuteronomy 6:7 says, "Talk about them [the commands of God] when you sit at home and when you walk along the road, when you lie down and when you get up."

How do we impress our children to love and follow God's commands? By talking about them with our children. How can our kids possibly know how to do something if we have never talked to them about it?

As my daughter is now 15, I realize that having a driver's license and driving a car is quickly approaching for her. Guess what? She has never driven a car before so how do I possibly expect her to know what to do?

A few weeks ago, I put her in my wife's car with me. (Did you notice whose car I used?) We went to an abandoned warehouse parking lot for the first lesson. I had to tell her how to adjust her seat, set the mirrors, put the car into drive, and how to use the blinkers and brakes without slamming me through the windshield! As she drove,

I gave her tips and suggestions and over the next hour she became more confident in her ability to drive.

That's how it is with the ways of God. Essentially, impressing faith on our children is about show and tell. We need to *show* them that we are in love with God by passionately, joyfully, and obediently following the ways of God ourselves, and then we need to *tell* them how to do it themselves.

The reason I personalize the Ten Commandments as I did was hopefully to provide you with a tool for show and tell with your children. I wanted you to see how we can and should personalize, talk about, and explain the ways of God to our children. If all we do is have them memorize the Ten Commandments, they may be able to recite them for a bit, but they may never know what they truly mean and why they should follow them.

I believe too many parents have taken their kids to church expecting the church to teach their kids the Ten Commandments. Unfortunately, the church is equally to blame because we take the kids and put them in a church program where they memorize the Ten Commandments. When the kids are able to recite the Ten Commandments at a closing program, we all applaud and walk away feeling good. But how many of those kids do you think will be able to repeat the Ten Commandments a year later? Two years later? Five years later? Not many at all. Why didn't they stick? Because we never talked about the Ten Commandments at home!

The ways of God were meant to be truths we discussed and lived out 24 hours a day, seven days a week. It's not like God has a quiz requiring us to recite the Ten Commandments before we enter heaven. We are called to be a people who "are" the Ten Commandments not simply a people who know them.

The Bigger Issue

While we should be living out and talking to our children about the ways of God, the bigger issue is that we are called as parents to be faith talkers! During the past 40-50 years, Christians have evolved into a people who don't talk about their faith outside of church. Some may say they don't talk about their faith publicly because they don't want to offend anyone, but how does that apply to your home? I don't think the reason why we aren't faith talking at home is because we are worried about offending our kids. As I work with parents, I have discovered there are two primary reasons why faith talk isn't happening in homes today.

Time

For many parents the issue is finding time for faith talk. Unfortunately, I think we make this harder than it needs to be. For many parents, they believe faith talk requires setting aside a specific time when the entire family will gather together around the kitchen table for an hour to read the Bible with a candle burning!

We think we need to find a time for faith talk, and yet our Bible verse does not teach that. The Bible simply says we are to engage in faith talk anytime and anywhere throughout our day.

Consider these suggestions:

- You have a short time of prayer in the morning with your kids before they head out the door to catch the school bus.
- You talk to your son about God's commandment on stealing in the van on the way home from school after he tells you that his lunch money was stolen from his backpack.
- You have a faith talk with your teen daughter on contentment at the mall over lunch as you watch all the other teenagers spending ridiculous amounts of money on trendy clothing.
- You pray in your car for the people you drove by who were recently in an accident and were getting medical assistance.
- You encounter your daughter crying in her bedroom because of false things other girls at school have been saying about her, and you decide to talk to her about seeking revenge versus staying true to who she is.

First of all, if we wait for the right time to have these talks, we will have missed the right time. The Bible is clear that our home should be the safest and easiest place to engage in faith talk. We shouldn't need to wait until we go to church to have faith talk. The home is intended to be the primary place where faith is lived, expressed, discussed, and

> # The home is intended to be the primary place where faith is lived, expressed, discussed, and nurtured.

nurtured. And we do have plenty of time and opportunity at home to engage in faith talk, whether it be in the morning, at mealtime, bedtime, and even in our cars.

Mealtime

Mealtime is always a great opportunity to engage in faith talk as a family. Whether you are in a restaurant or at your kitchen table, you can use mealtime as an opportunity to discuss your highs and lows from the day or your joys and concerns. Another thing you can discuss at mealtime is if anyone experienced any "God moments" that day? A "God moment" may be something as simple as a 10-minute walk you had during lunch, or it could entail a significant experience that happened that day. Some families also have a "God-talk" box in the middle of their table that has a series of faith talk questions in it like:

- What does the symbol of the cross mean to you?
- What is one of your favorite memories of attending a church service?
- What is a good or bad memory you have of Sunday school?
- What is your favorite part of the Lord's Prayer?
- What does the phrase, "unless you become like a little child you cannot enter the kingdom of heaven" mean to you?
- What is one of your greatest fears?
- What is an act of service that you would like to do someday?
- Who is someone with a strong faith that you admire?

Keep a notepad and pen close to the "God-talk" box so anyone can add future faith talk questions.

Morning Time

Most families find themselves in a rush trying to get ready and out the door each morning; yet, a simple opportunity for faith talk can happen each morning—the prayer huddle. Essentially, all you do is quickly huddle together as a family, pick one person to say a short prayer and/or blessing, and then put your hands in the middle. When the prayer is done, everyone says together, "Yeah God!" Another suggestion for faith talk in the morning is to keep a topical Bible or daily devotional book setting where your kids normally eat breakfast. Some mornings you won't have time because everyone is running late, but other mornings you will find you have time to go through one of the topics and/or daily devotions as you eat breakfast together.

Car Time

In today's fast-paced world, one of the best opportunities we may have to engage in faith talk happens when we are traveling in the vehicle together. When my daughter was younger, I loved the time we had on the way to and from her school because this was time when we talked together, prayed, and listen to Christian music. Another great thing to do in the car is to listen to Christian comedians like Tim Hawkins because they can give you some great things to laugh about followed by a great message.

Many families also use car time for prayer. When on the way to school, they pray for the things of the day as well as their teachers and anything else going on in the community or world. The way home from work/school becomes a chance to pray for the things that transpired during the day and to give God thanks for getting us through another day!

And finally, as I mentioned earlier, I truly believe car time is a great time to listen to Christian music together. We live in a great time where there is Christian music of every style. Find an artist your kids enjoy, and crank it up in the car. Singing praises to our God with your children is a wonderful way to connect.

Bedtime

Bedtime is one of the most intimate times for faith talk. Every evening my wife and I engage in faith talk with our daughter, but we each do it differently. For my wife, each evening as she gives Malyn a hug, she will say the following blessing over her: "May the Lord bless you and keep you. May He make His face shine on you and be gracious to you. May He look upon you with favor and give you peace. In the name of the Father and the Son and the Holy Spirit. Amen."[25] When Maria is done saying the blessing over Malyn, it is now my time to pray with her. Sometimes we will pray in the living room, while other times I will go into her bedroom and we will talk for a while before we pray together. Before our prayer time, I will usually ask questions like: What were your highs today? What were your lows? What are you glad/thankful for? What concerns do you have? No matter what has happened that day, we always end the day with a blessing and prayer.

Bedtime is also a great time to read Bible stories to your children and even listen to nighttime devotional CDs together. The nice thing about Bible reading, prayer, blessings, and faith talk at bedtime is that it can easily become a routine your children expect every evening.

As D6 parents, we have been called to lead our children to life through faith in Jesus Christ that is grounded in the way we talk about God anytime and all the time. Let's seize the moments that God provides for faith talk. Instead of trying to make faith talk happen, we should simply be ready for it whenever a situation arises that calls for faith talk. If you have more than one child, don't make it difficult on yourself. Wait for the moments God provides for you to engage in faith talk with each child independently as you go through your day/week. For one child, it may happen in the morning over breakfast, while for the other, it will happen at bedtime. Some nights my daughter wants to open the Bible on a specific topic, while other nights she just wants to pray quickly because she is exhausted. I simply take advantage of the times and opportunities God presents for me to have faith talk with her.

Know How & Tools

The second barrier many parents have for engaging in faith talk with their children is that they are concerned they are ill-equipped. In other words, they are not sure they have the know-how.

When it comes to talking about God's ways, I think we all need to admit that we are out of our element and we aren't experts, nor do we have God all figured out.

However, we do have access to God; therefore, we can, at any point and time, come to know God and His ways better. And the good news is that God wants to reveal His ways to us! God isn't trying to hide anything from us nor does He want to make things difficult for us. Remember, God wants things to go well for us, therefore, the last thing God is going to do, as our Father, is make it hard for His kids to succeed. That's why God has provided a variety of tools to help us engage in faith talk anytime, all the time.

Creation

God's wonderful and awe-inspiring creation is one of the best resources for engaging in faith talk with our children. Go to the zoo and talk about God's creativity and sense of humor when you look at all the animals God has created. As you watch the ocean waves crash, you can talk about the awesome power of God. While staring at the stars at night, you can talk about how big our God is. When you see a snake, you can discuss why God describes Satan as a snake.

God's creation surrounds us every day. When we slow down and see it, creation provides all sorts of topics for us.

If you're looking for an easy faith talk activity just do what my daughter and I did this summer. On a specific day, we each took the digital camera and simply took pictures of things we were drawn to. Then that evening we went through the pictures and talked about each picture and how we saw or experienced an aspect of God in each picture.

God's Word

It only makes sense that a great option for faith talk includes God in the conversation. The Bible is God's Living Word to us; therefore, we are involving God in our faith talk whenever we are using the Bible.

The primary question I receive from parents is how do I use the Bible to have faith talk. While many parents would agree that using the Bible would be helpful, most are intimidated by the Bible. Consider tools to help you use the Bible for faith talk.

1. Start with a children's Bible. We live in a great day where there are Bibles for nearly every age. We have story Bibles for children, teen Bibles for students, Bibles for girls and boys, and I was even told there is a scratch and sniff Bible! While I'm not sure where I stand on the scratch and sniff Bible, I will say that I absolutely recommend parents use age appropriate Bibles with their children. Use different Bibles, but as you do, be sure to write and make notes in them as you go through them as these will become more important in the years to come.

Right now my daughter loves her new Fellowship of Christian Athlete's Bible because she is a very strong cross country and track runner. The FCA Bible provides a lot of good stories and analogies for athletes, which really connects with her at this stage in her life.

2. Use topical Bibles. As you move beyond picture Bibles, you will now find myriad of topical Bibles as well. The nice thing about topical Bibles is that they provide a list of topics for you to pick from that then lead you to passages from God's Word on that topic. Recently, my daughter was worried about a few different things going on in her life, so we opened her topical Bible and went to the passages about the topic of worry. A few minutes later, we had received some great advice and counsel from God about how we should handle our worries.

3. Get a Concordance. Finally, every family should have a concordance, which is something you can pick up online or at your local Christian bookstore. A concordance provides a list of words alphabetically and where these words appear in all the books, chapters, and verses of the Bible. Many times we find ourselves in situations where we know the Bible has something to say about temptation, but we can't remember what or where it is. By using your concordance, you can look up the word *temptation* and find the verses where it appears. Many times you will learn even more than you expected.

Prayer

Again, prayer is faith talk to and with God. Through prayer, we are talking openly and honestly with each other and with God. In my book, *Faith Begins at Home Prayer*, I shared many ways that families can engage in prayer at mealtime, bedtime, morning time, and anytime; yet, again I feel we make prayer more difficult than it needs to be.

There are many ways to pray. We should create an environment at home where prayer happens anytime and all the time. We musn't wait until our kids go to bed to pray with them. If they need prayer on the way to school, then pray with them on the way to school.

> **We should create an environment at home where prayer happens anytime and all the time.**

Church

I love going to church with my wife and daughter. Yet what I love the most is our car ride home and lunch after church because that is the time when we talk about church. I love hearing what my daughter and wife appreciated. We also take some time to go through the bulletin to see if there is anything we need to do or pray for. Going to church and participating in church programs provide many great things for us to talk about at home.

So there you have it! As you can see, we really have no excuse not to engage in faith talk because we have time, know-how, and plenty to talk about. So let's get started faith talking!

Small Group Discussion Questions

1. What type of faith talk did you experience growing up?

2. Who were the people that talked to you about God and God's ways?

3. Who are the primary people in your life today with whom you have faith talk?

4. How much faith talk currently happens in your home?

5. What are some ways that you could engage in faith talk at:

   a. Bedtime

   b. Morning time

   c. Mealtime

   d. Car time

   e. Other?

6. Which tool helps you engage in faith talk the most?

   a. Prayer

   b. The Bible

   c. Nature/creation

   d. The church

7. Which tool for faith talk would work best for each of your children?

Letter to . . .

Greetings, my friend.

So how are things going for you? Last week we talked about specific things we want to impress upon our children so that they will know and follow these principles for the rest of their lives. Now the question becomes how do we do this? Obviously, as we discussed, it starts with us knowing, loving, and living those things ourselves; but what is the next best thing you can do to lead your kids to life through faith in Christ? It's actually really simple—talk about God with your kids at home.

Being a Christian is an ongoing journey. Each day is a day when we can learn and experience new things about God, which gives us plenty to talk about. Yet for some reason many people think the only place to talk about God is at church. If you truly love someone, you don't talk with him/her only one hour a week. It seems like we can talk to our kids about everything from sports to school activities and even relationships, but when it comes to talking about God, we seem to shy away from that. If you're kids are going to learn about God, they need to hear it from you.

The thing I hear most from parents, when it comes to faith talk, is that they don't have time and don't know how. Let's deal with both of these. When it comes to not having time to engage in faith talk, my answer to that is simply: That's a bunch of bologna! Seriously, if you have time to talk with them about their ball game, you have time to engage in faith talk. For many they think they have to set aside time for faith talk where we all sit down together at the kitchen table for an hour reading our Bibles and engaging in faith talk. That's not my picture of faith talk. My picture of faith talk is something that just happens naturally throughout the course of your day. It may happen in the car, at night, during a meal, or over the cell phone. Malyn and I have faith talks using text messaging.

Second, when it comes to knowing how, I realize that you may not feel equipped to have a faith talk with your wife or children. Well the good news is this: They are no better equipped for it than you are! And if you think you must have all the right answers or be some sort of Bible know-it-all before you have faith talk, then you will never have faith talk because we will never know it all when it comes to God. To be honest, some of the best faith talk is when we talk about what we don't know or understand about God and His ways.

Thankfully, God has provided us tools so that we can get to know Him better. I encourage you to use these tools so you can feel better equipped.

1. With your children, use story Bibles targeted for their ages. Since you have two kids, I would encourage you to get one for each, and then let your older son hand his Bible down to your daughter when he is ready to move on to his next Bible. Tell your son that you are going to hand his Bible down to his sister and with him write notes to her as you go through the stories. When your daughter gets the Bible and begins reading it for herself, she will also have some fun notes from you and her brother.

2. As your kids get older use topical Bibles because then you can choose a topic to explore and/or learn about each time you read it.

3. And finally, be sure to get a concordance, which is an alphabetical listing of words found in the Bible and where they appear. For example, you may want to find what the Bible has

to say about worry. Using your concordance you will be able to find all the places where the word *worry* occurs in the Bible.

In addition to using the Bible to engage in faith talk, I also encourage you to take advantage of God's wonderful creation. Simply talk about God when you are outside enjoying the lake, taking a walk, or watching a snow storm. Each day we can see things that give us a great God moment.

I also encourage you to have faith talk through prayer with your kids as well as through things you will do at church together. Prayer is probably the easiest form of faith talk. When we go to church we will also hear and learn all sorts of things we can talk about as a family when we get home.

So here's your homework: Think about how you will engage in faith talk on a regular basis with your spouse and each of your children. Recognize that it will be different for each one based on what works for him/her.

Don't put pressure on yourself to do this, but simply look for opportunities when you can do this. Seize those opportunities.

Have fun and enjoy faith talking!

In Christ,

Mark

Chapter 7
Walk the Walk

Looking Back . . . (Repetition of the Law)

- A good parent is someone who leads his/her children to life not death.
- Deuteronomy 6 provides a roadmap for how to be a parent who leads his/her children to life, which is why we want to be D6 parents.
- D6 parents are "careful to obey" the ways of God so that "it may go well" and so that we may "increase" as a family.
- D6 parents recognize they cannot outsource or abdicate the responsibility of spiritual formation of their children to the church.
- D6 parents know and believe there is only one, true God—Father-Son-Holy Spirit—and they live in a loving relationship with God.
- D6 parents engage in faith talk anytime, all the time.

For our 20th wedding anniversary, my wife surprised me with framed newspaper articles of Michael Jordan and the Chicago Bulls' last championship win. I am a huge Chicago Bulls fan, so when they were winning championships, I put up paraphernalia and newspaper articles everywhere. It was a real treat to get this gift so I can relive the glory days with them hanging in my office (because my wife won't let me hang them anywhere else in the house).

Now I have also discovered that guys aren't the only ones who do this because my wife has grown to love the art of cooking more and more. As a result, she watches cooking shows as often as she can and we have collected a wide array of cookbooks, cooking utensils, pots and pans, and an ever-growing assortment of cooking "tools."

My wife also loves to dance and listen to music, which is something she learned by dancing and listening to music with her mother as they cleaned the house together. Now my daughter has also grown to love music and dancing as well. Lord, help me!

What's my point? We tend to showcase what we love through the things we have and do in our homes.

A Youth Ministry Trade Secret

I probably shouldn't give this away, but here's a secret I learned in youth ministry: If you want to truly know what was going on in a teenager's life, look at his/her bedroom. After five minutes, I knew what their hobbies were, who their favorite personalities or sports teams were, and theirs musical interests.

I realize that thanks to Facebook, I could now probably get much of the same information without having to see their bedroom; but there is still something more you can learn by getting into their home.

In addition to what I learned about the teenager, I also learned a lot about his/her family by spending time in the home. Home visits reveal if a family is into pets, sports, music, entertaining, watching TV, as well as many other things.

Now I don't want you to think this is only what pastors or youth pastors are doing when they come to your home, but I think we must admit that what we have in our homes reveals a lot about who we are and what we are into as a family.

Deuteronomy 6:8-9 says, "Tie them as symbols on your hands and bind them on your foreheads. Write them on the doorframes of your houses and on your gates."

For me, this portion of Deuteronomy 6 is pointing out another way we impress faith on our children—through the way we take God with us wherever we go and through the things we have and do at home.

Tie Them, Bind Them

Faith and godly living is something you can do all the time; I learned that while growing up

> **Another way we impress faith on our children—through the way we take God with us wherever we go and through the things we have and do at home.**

at Bible camp. At camp, you truly encounter what it is to "walk the walk" in a Christ-like way, 24/7 for the length of your stay there. And that's why many people love going to spend a week at camp because they are able retreat from the noise and temptations of the real world and simply immerse themselves in an intentional Christian environment for a week.

However, towards the end of the week we always focused on "reentry." When I was asked to give the reentry message/challenge. I focused on two things I believe are the essence of what Moses meant when he told his people to "tie them" and "bind them."

Don't Be Ashamed

Obviously, if something is tied to your hands or tattooed to your forehead, it would be something others would notice! When Moses instructs us to "tie them as symbols on your hands and bind them on your foreheads," I believe he means we are called to "wear" or demonstrate to others through the way we live, following the ways of God. In other words, we aren't called to hide or be ashamed, but we are called to showcase boldly our choice to follow God.

My dad loved music. He was not only an incredible musician who played any instrument, but he also had an out–of–this–world voice with a built in amplifier.

My dad was never ashamed of his love of music. If there were a piano in the room, he began playing it. Whenever we visited a church, within moments of the first song, people turned around to see the guy with the great voice.

Similarly, I'm not embarrassed to say that I'm in love with God or that my family and I have chosen to live our lives following the ways of God. In fact, I find it difficult to withhold that information or act and live in such a way to reflect I'm not in love with or following God. Does this mean I'm perfect or better than anyone else? Absolutely not, and yet I will say that living according to the standard of loving God and His ways and loving others as He loves them is not a standard that I'm ashamed to admit or live by. What other standard would you rather live by?

I don't know how it happened, but somehow under the banner of "political correctness," we feel we cannot show or say we are in love with God or that we are a people seeking to live according to God's ways. And what makes things even worse is that in our fear, timidity, or bashfulness, we then lead our children to be afraid, timid, or bashful to love God and live according to His ways.

Do I want my daughter to be timid, afraid, or bashful of her faith? Do I want her to be afraid, timid, or bashful to live according to the ways of God? I want her to be bold, strong, and fearless when it comes to saying she is in love with God. And I want her to have a bold, strong, and fearless faith that will guide her to make bold, strong, and fearless decisions as she goes through life. Therefore if I want her to have a bold, strong, and fearless relationship with God, then I need to have a bold, strong, and fearless faith that I'm not ashamed of.

"I am not ashamed of the gospel, because it is the power of God that brings salvation to everyone who believes" (Romans 1:6).

Remain

I also believe, "tie them as symbols on your hands and bind them on your foreheads" implies an aspect of permanence when it comes to doing life God's way. In other words, if something is tied to your hands or tattooed on your forehead, it's not going away!

One of my favorite portions of Scripture appears in John 15. To set the backdrop, Jesus has been on a three-year journey with His disciples where he was teaching and showing them how to live God's way. Unfortunately, His next step involved leaving them to defeat death on the cross for all of us. Jesus is very close to His disciples because they have done life together for more than three years; therefore, Jesus, knowing what lies ahead, decides to spend some final time with His most fully-devoted followers before He will be separated from them. Obviously, what Jesus shares with them is going to be very important and from the heart just like some of the final words my dad shared with me before he went to his heavenly home.

In a truly unique portion of the Bible, Jesus repeats one word 11 times in seven verses. Nowhere else in the Bible does Jesus repeat himself this much, which means he was clearly trying to make a point. What was that word? Take a look:

<u>Remain</u> in me, as I also <u>remain</u> in you. No branch can bear fruit by itself; it must <u>remain</u> in the vine. Neither can you bear fruit unless you <u>remain</u> in me. I am the vine; you are the branches. If you <u>remain</u> in me and I in you, you will bear much fruit; apart from me you can do nothing. If you do not <u>remain</u> in me, you are like a branch that is thrown away and withers; such branches are picked up, thrown into the fire and burned. If you <u>remain</u> in me and my words <u>remain</u> in you, ask whatever you wish, and it will be done for you. This is to my Father's glory, that you bear much fruit, showing yourselves to be my disciples. As the Father has loved me, so have I loved you. Now <u>remain</u> in my love. If you keep my commands, you will <u>remain</u> in my love, just as I have kept my Father's commands and <u>remain</u> in his love. I have told you this so that my joy may be in you and that your joy may be complete (John 15:4-11, underlining added).

Eleven times Jesus admonishes his disciples to "remain." Why would Jesus want to make sure His disciples understood this before He left?

To be perfectly honest, choosing to do life God's way is actually an easy choice to make, especially when you come to understand that God's way leads to "increase" and "enjoying long (eternal) life." However, the decision to do life God's way is more than a one-time decision. It also requires an ongoing commitment through life.

Do you want things to go well for you as a family? Remain. Do you want to increase as a family? Remain. Do you want to bear fruit as a family? Remain. Do you want to enjoy long, everlasting life as a family? Remain.

So as to help you remain in the ways of God I would simply encourage you to live according to WWJHMD. What is WWJHMD? In the 1980s, a bracelet became a widespread phenomenon, appearing in every shape, size, and color that simply had four letters on it: WWJD. Those four letters stood for What Would Jesus Do? People purchased and wore these bracelets because they reminded them to constantly think and ask themselves: What would Jesus do?

I too purchased and wore these bracelets, but I always wanted to add two letters: WWJHMD, which simply stands for What Would Jesus Have Me Do? For me, "remaining" simply comes down to continually asking and living according to What Would Jesus Have Me Do in all situations and circumstances. For instance:

- When you are cut off on the interstate and someone honks and points that one finger at you, remember: What Would Jesus Have Me Do?
- When you have a chance to take revenge on someone who has hurt you in the past, remember: What Would Jesus Have Me Do?
- When you are in a situation where you could engage in adultery or pornography, remember: What Would Jesus Have Me Do?
- When you have a chance to slander a co-worker or manipulate a work situation s to get ahead at the expense of someone else, What Would Jesus Have Me Do?
- When you see an elderly person struggling to put groceries into the car, What Would Jesus Have Me Do?

When we are truly doing what Jesus would have us do at home, work, school, in our neighborhoods, and at our churches, we have then truly "tied" and "bound" the ways of God on our hearts.

Write Them

When Moses writes, "write them on the doorframes of your houses and on your gates," I am instantly taken back to the time when we were preparing to send our daughter to Kindergarten. Obviously, since she was and is our one and only child, we didn't have any experience to draw from. When the preparation letter came informing us how to prepare our daughter for Kindergarten, we did everything it said to the maximum.

One of the things listed was to put Malyn's name on her items, including clothing so that she could always know and/or find the items that were hers. Maria and I went crazy labeling everything! We began by putting Malyn's name on all of her shirts, jackets, and boots. We continued to label things like her lunch box and backpack, but did we stop there? Oh no. we labeled her pads of paper, crayons, glue stick, and even eraser! We were labeling fools because we wanted everyone to know whose items these were.

In a similar, but not so extreme way, I think as God's people we have been called to attach God's name to the things we have so we don't forget whose they are.

In Deuteronomy 6:10-11 Moses writes, "When the LORD your God brings you into the land he swore to your fathers, to Abraham, Isaac and Jacob, to give you—a land with large, flourishing cities you did not build, houses filled with all kinds of good things you did not provide, wells you did not dig, and vineyards and olive groves you did not plant—then when you eat and are satisfied."

Whenever I read that I find myself identifying with it because I live in a city I didn't build, drink water from a well I didn't dig, have trees in my yard I didn't plant, and I have a house filled will all sorts of stuff that I have no idea where it came from!

Verse 12 says, "Be careful that you do not forget the LORD." It's so easy in today's world, where we have so much, to forget the one who has provided all this for us. Maybe we need to get out our label machines!

Here are a few things you can do to "write them on the doorframes of your houses and gates" so that you won't forget.

1. Get a Joshua 24 rock. In Joshua 24, after the people had declared that they would "love and obey God," Joshua took a rock and said to the people, "This stone will be a witness against us. . . . It will be a witness against you if you are untrue to your God" (verse 27). As a family, find a few individual rocks, as well as a large family rock. Put the individual rocks in places where you will see them daily. For kids that may be in their book bag, school desk, or locker. For adults that may be in their purse, bathroom, or office desk. Take the large family rock and put it in a place of prominence in your home. You can write Joshua 24 on your rock. Every time you see it, it will be a reminder to you that everything you have is a gift from God.

2. Keep the Word of God out and with you. Again the Bible is the Living Word of God, so it should be something we have with us everywhere. I once challenged my church to go home and collect all the Bibles, count how many they had, and then place them around their home prominently. One family came to me the following week and said, "Pastor Mark, you'll never guess how many Bibles we found—27! Do you know how hard it was to find 27 places to put the Bible in our home? We now have a Bible next to each toilet!"

For parents who work, I strongly encourage you to take a Bible to work with you. Don't be ashamed to keep it at your desk or in your car. Trust me, you will be glad to have access to God's wisdom and counsel when you are at work!.

3. Set a Jesus seat. To remember that Jesus is with us at home some families set an extra spot at the table as a reminder that Jesus is with them. This is a great way to also continually remind your kids that Jesus is alive and well!

4. Other God reminders. We live in a day where you can have reminders of God on your computer, hanging on your walls, as the jewelry you wear, hanging from your rear view mirror, and on your iPod! What we have displayed in our offices and homes demonstrates what and whom we love.

Small Group Discussion Questions

1. How timid or bold would you say you are in your walk with God? What would help you be more bold, strong, or fearless?

2. What are some of the stereotypes that exist about Christians? How accurate are they? How can we best overcome them?

3. What are some things that make it difficult for you to "remain" doing life God's way? What helps you remain?

4. How did the admonishment, "be careful that you do not forget the LORD" impact you?

5. How do you keep God and His ways in the forefront of your mind and life?

6. How does your home reflect what/whom you love? How could it?

Letter To . . .

Hey my friend,

I am on a flight to New York for another weekend of speaking, but I just had a great experience with my daughter Malyn yesterday. She had another cross-country meet. Although she is only a freshman, she has been battling with one other girl to be the top runner on her team. Malyn always gets out to a fast start and is usually leading the other girl after the first mile, but then slowly, in the final mile, her teammate overtakes her. Malyn usually ends up finishing just behind her. Well in yesterday's race the same thing happened. Malyn was out in front, but then at the end of the second mile, her teammate passed her. You could see the look of discouragement come over her face. They then went out of sight; but when the returned into our sight to begin the stretch run to the finish line, Malyn had retaken the lead and ended up finishing just ahead of her teammate! Obviously, I was the proudest dad in the world, who also had lost my voice cheering for her. When I saw her after the race, I simply said, "What happened?" She responded, "I'm not exactly sure really. Normally, when my friend passes me I get discouraged feeling like I've hit the same wall I always hit and can't get passed; but when she passed me today, I decided to pray, over and over again, for God to give me strength to get past this discouragement. The next thing you know I was passing her!"

Seriously, dude, that's as good as it gets for me as a dad. Having a kid that turns to God to give her strength when she is facing hardship or difficulty.

As you and I have discussed, I'm not a fan of hypcocrites. A lot of people can "talk the talk" or go to church and say they are Christians. A real Christian is someone who doesn't just talk the talk, but also walks the walk. Malyn isn't a Christian only at church or when it's safe and convenient for her to do so, she's doing it at school and in the middle of a cross-country race! That's our next step to be the type of men, husbands, and fathers who live our lives God's way, not only at home but also at work and at play. So what does that look like?

Again it's probably easier than you realize, just remember WWJHMD. What is WWJHMD? It stands for What Would Jesus Have Me Do. That's really all we need at home, work, and play is to live according to what would Jesus have you do. You need to run your business and make your decisions according to what would Jesus have you do. In your dealings with people, handle them according to what would Jesus have you do. And when you are tempted, ask, what would Jesus have me do?

Seriously, if you think about it and really did what Jesus wanted you to do in every situation, chances are your life would go much better. It's when we don't do what Jesus wants us to do that we end up in trouble.

To help you do this you need to remind yourself to live according to WWJHMD. Here are some things that have helped me. I have a small cross that hangs from my rear view mirror that reminds me to drive and treat people who drive around me according to WWJHMD. For awhile I wore a leather bracelet with WWJHMD engraved on it. Another thing we do as a family is to keep our Bibles out around our house, which not only reminds us to live according to WWJHMD, but it also keeps us reading the Word of God whenever we feel like it. We have also occasionally written a specific Scripture verse on a note card and put in on our refrigerator, or we have even written it directly on our bathroom mirror.

And finally, because I know where you work doesn't have a lot of room for anything I would suggest you get a hand sized rock and write Joshua 24 on it. Why? Because in Joshua 24, after the people have made a declaration that they will serve and follow the Lord, Joshua responded by taking a large rock and saying, "This stone will be a witness against us. . . . It will be a witness against you if you are untrue to your God." Find a rock and place it where you work so that every time you see it you are reminded to be a Faith@Home focused guy.

So there you have it. Let's be guys who don't just talk the talk when it comes to following God and His ways, but let's walk the walk as well. Love ya, bro.

In Christ,

Mark

Conclusion

A Final Friendship Letter

Greetings my friend,

Well here is the last letter I will be writing to you as I have finally completed writing the book God has called me to write. What a journey this has been; and yet, I feel like this is more of the starting line rather than finish. We've really only just begun our journey together as friends. I want you to know that even though my formal letters may be coming to an end, I'm still here for you over the long haul. Thanks for welcoming, reading, and responding to my letters. I can't wait to see how God is going to transform and strengthen you and your family in the days, weeks, months, and years ahead.

In one of Jesus' final conversations with his disciples Jesus says, "You are my friends if you do what I command. I no longer call you servants, because a servant does not know his master's business. Instead, I have called you friends, for everything that I learned from my Father I have made known to you" (John 15:14-16). My prayer is that through these letters you have received a "repetition of the law" whereby you have reconnected with Jesus as your Savior, who gave His life so you and your children and children's children "may enjoy long life," and best friend, so that your life beginning now and forevermore "may go well with you."

In Deuteronomy 6, we have a parenting roadmap that can lead each and every one of us to be great parents. It doesn't matter what your past relationship with God has been or what type of parent you have been up to this point. Through D6, we each have the opportunity to be great parents, who through the guidance of God, can lead our children to eternal life! We have been encouraged, challenged, and admonished by God to "be careful to obey" so that "it may go well" and so that we may "increase" as a family. God wants the very best for you, your children, and your grandchildren to come; yet, as friends of Jesus we need to "do what He commands" in Deuteronomy 6 which is:

As D6 parents, we need to align our mission as a family with God's mission so that it may go well with us and that we may increase in love, joy, peace, patience, kindness, goodness, faithfulness, gentleness, and self-control.

As D6 parents, we need to establish our home as the primary place where faith is going to be lived out, expressed, and nurtured, not outsourcing or abdicating this responsibility to the church.

As D6 parents, we need to live in an authentic loving relationship with THE one, true God—Father-Son-Holy Spirit—because our children will love who we love.

As D6 parents, we need to permanently impress the commands/ways of God on our children so that they will influence the decisions our children will make in life.

As D6 parents, we need to engage in faith talk with our children anytime and all the time so that conversation with God in and through prayer, Bible reading, and worship happens casually and naturally.

As D6 parents, we need to live out our faith not only at home but also at work and wherever else we go because doing life God's way is not an obligation or church centric thing; it is a 24-hour-a-day, seven-day-a-week way of life.

There you have it. Let me now conclude our journey together, which is more of a launching point for you as a D6 family, with the following blessing that my dad would always say at the end of any sermon: My friend, may the Lord bless you and keep you. May the Lord make His face shine on you and be gracious to you. May the Lord look upon you with favor and give you peace. In the name of the Father, Son and Holy Spirit. Amen.

In Christ and your friend,

Mark

Endnotes

[1] Jim Collins, *Good To Great*, (Harper Collins Publishers, 2001, New York, NY) 6, 11.

[2] Jim Burns, *Confident Parenting*, (Bethany House Publishing, 2007, Minneapolis, MN) 59.

[3] Merton P. Strommen and Irene A. Strommen, *Five Cries of Parents* (Minneapolis: Youth and Fmaily Institue, 1993), p. 134.

[4] Peter L. Benson, *Catholic High Schools: Their Impact on Low-Income Students* (Washington, DC: National Catholic Educational Association [NCEA], 1986), p. 99.

[5] Peter L. Benson and Carolyn H. Eklin, *Effective Christian Education: A National Study of Protestant Congregations* (Minneapolis: Search Institute, 1990), p. 46.

[6] George Barna, *Transforming Children Into Spiritual Champions*, Gospel Light, Ventura, CA, 2003, p. 78.

[7] Early Childhood Education Study, Search Institute, Minneapolis, MN.

[8] Merton P. Strommen and Richard A. Hardel, *Passing on the Faith*, Saint Mary's Press, Winona, MN, 2000 p. 14.

[9] Dean, Kenda Creasy. *Almost Christian - What the Faith of Our Teenagers Is Telling the American Church.* (New York, Oxford University Press, 2010).

[10] Rick Lawrence, *Jesus-Centered Youth Ministry* (Loveland, CO: Group Publishing, 2007), 33, 46.

[11] George Barna (Researcher) www.barna.org/barna-update/article/16-teensnext-gen/147-most-twentysomethings-put-christianity-on-the-shelf-following-spiritually-active-teen-years.

[12] T. C. Pinkney (Vice-President of Southern Baptist Convention) reports that 70 percent of teenagers involved in church youth groups stop attending church within two years of their high school graduation. (T.C. Pinkney, *Report to the Southern Baptist Convention Executive Committee*, Nashville, Tennessee, September 18, 2001). In another study from the Southern Baptist Council on Family Life, they found

88 percent of the children raised in evangelical homes leave church at the age of 18, never to return. (*Southern Baptist Council on Family Life report to Annual Meeting of the Southern Baptist Convention*, 2002, www.sbcannualmeeting.net/sbc02/newsroom/newspage.asp?ID=261)

[13]Reggie McNeal, *The Present Future* (Jossey-Bass, San Francisco, CA, 2003), p. 4.) citing youth ministry specialist Dawson MacAlister.

[14]George Barna (Researcher) *Revolution* (Tyndale House Publishers, Carol Stream, IL, 2005), p. 48-49).

[15]David Kinnaman, *UnChristian* (Grand Rapids MI: Zondervan Publishing, 2008), p. 42. Used by permission.

[16]Merton P. Strommen and Richard A. Hardel, *Passing on the Faith*, Saint Mary's Press, Winona, MN, 2000 p. 29.

[17]Burns, Jim, *Confident Parenting*, Bethany House Publishing, 2007, Minneapolis, MN p.40.

[18]Richard Ross, *Student Ministry and the Supremacy of Christ*, Crossbooks Publishing, 2009, Bloomington, IN, 40.

[19]Richard Ross, *Student Ministry and the Supremacy of Christ*, Crossbooks Publishing, 2009, Bloomington, IN, 148.

[20]Denton, Christian Smith with Melinda Lundquist. *Soul Searching: The Religious and Spiritual Lives of American Teenagers.* New York: Oxford University Press, 2005.

[21]Jim Burns, *Confident Parenting*, Bethany House Publishing, 2007, Minneapolis, MN, 61.

[22]Christian Smith with Melinda Lundquist Denton, *Soul Searching: The Religious and Spiritual Lives of American Teenagers* (New York: Oxford University Press, 2005), 162-63.

[23]Marjorie Thompson, *The Family as Forming Center* (Nashville, TN: Upper Room Books, 1996), p. 144.

[24]Dolores Curran, "Family Ministry," in *Family Ministry* (Minneapolis: Winston Press, 1980), p. 17.

[25]Numbers 6:24-26.

Family Mission Statement Template

DAD

My non-negotiables

_____
_____
_____
_____
_____
_____

MOM

My non-negotiables

_____
_____
_____
_____
_____

KIDS

My non-negotiables

_____
_____
_____
_____
_____
_____

FAMILY

Our master list of non-negotiables

_____
_____
_____
_____

Our Family Mission Statement

_____
_____
_____
_____
_____
_____

Also available
from Mark Holmen

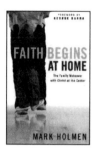

Faith Begins At Home
The Family Makeover with Christ at the Center

Faith Begins @ Home Dad
Faith Begins @ Home Mom
Faith Begins @ Home Devotions
Faith Begins @ Home Prayer

Visit Mark at www.faithathome.com.

EVERY MARRIAGE
MATTERS TO GOD.

After years of counseling engaged and married couples, the Rienows realized that most Christian couples didn't know WHY God had brought them together! *Visionary Marriage* will reveal that God does have a plan and a purpose for marriage and family in the Bible. The focus is on the big-picture purpose for marriage, and the goal of being successful once understanding the purpose.

Ideal for small group study with discussion questions at the end of each chapter.

Visionary Marriage by Rob and Amy Rienow $12.99
Group discounts available

(ⁿ) randall house   D6family.com   800.877.7030

D6 Devotional Magazines
for the entire family!

D6 Devotional Magazines are unique because they are the only brand of devotional magazines where the entire family studies the same Bible theme at the same time.

Think about how long it would take you to track down all of the resources for each member of your family to connect with God on the same topic. Who has that kind of time? We do! It's not that we have nothing else to do, we are just passionate about D6. So look no further, we have created the resource for which you are looking, and it works!

D6 Devotional Magazines are full-color, interactive, fun, and exciting tools to connect with God and with each other.

Subscribe now!
800.877.7030
D6family.com